grief recovery
for teens

letting go of painful emotions
with body-based practices

CORAL POPOWITZ, MSW

"Regardless of age or background, each of us will experience grief during our lifetime. In *Grief Recovery for Teens*, Coral Popowitz shares dozens of things teens can do to find comfort, peace, and renewed hope. Grief hurts. Thankfully, Coral shows teens that they can indeed move forward to find happiness once again."

—**Neil Willenson**, founder of One Heartland for children affected by HIV/AIDS, and cofounder of Camp Hometown Heroes, a free national summer camp for children of fallen US service members

"Coral has written a highly relevant, much-needed book for the adolescent population. Her writing connects strongly with the youth of today challenged by their own grief and loss. Her approach, backed by strong, current research in the field, provides an individualized method for understanding and dealing with the very real physical, psychological, and emotional aspects of these difficult and potentially destabilizing life experiences. Her use of a holistic mind-body framework is presented in a truly accessible way. The important information on the adolescent brain and body; how these can be affected by our life experiences; and tools for managing these are well organized. This book offers teens compassionate understanding of—and the tools to work through—their unique experiences, not only for managing the loss of a loved one, but also for a variety of life stressors faced by our developing teens today."

—**Wendy L. Baker, MSW, LICSW**, cofounder of Family Circle Counseling in St. Paul, MN, adjunct faculty member at University of St. Thomas, and educator and consultant in areas of attachment, trauma, and adoption

"*Grief Recovery for Teens* is a comprehensive resource offering delicate balance between clear wisdom, concrete activities, and heartfelt stories. Coral covers the impact on mind, body, and heart during the grief experience as she helps teens make the adjustment toward understanding their lives after a death. Her writing is compassionate, informative, and practical. *Grief Recovery for Teens* reads as the wise advice of a true friend, and opens the reader to the honest and forthright conversations needed after a death."

> —**Peter Willig, LMFT, FT**, clinical director and COO of the Children's Bereavement Center; licensed marriage and family therapist; and fellow in thanatology with over twenty-five years of clinical experience

the *i*nstant help
solutions series

Young people today need mental health resources more than ever. That's why New Harbinger created the **Instant Help Solutions Series** especially for teens. Written by leading psychologists, physicians, and professionals, these evidence-based self-help books offer practical tips and strategies for dealing with a variety of mental health issues and life challenges teens face, such as depression, anxiety, bullying, eating disorders, trauma, and self-esteem problems.

Studies have shown that young people who learn healthy coping skills early on are better able to navigate problems later in life. Engaging and easy-to-use, these books provide teens with the tools they need to thrive—at home, at school, and on into adulthood.

This series is part of the **New Harbinger Instant Help Books** imprint, founded by renowned child psychologist Lawrence Shapiro. For a complete list of books in this series, visit newharbinger.com.

grief recovery
for **teens**

letting go of **painful emotions**
with **body-based practices**

CORAL POPOWITZ, MSW

Instant Help Books
An Imprint of New Harbinger Publications, Inc.

Publisher's Note

This publication is designed to provide accurate and authoritative information in regard to the subject matter covered. It is sold with the understanding that the publisher is not engaged in rendering psychological, financial, legal, or other professional services. If expert assistance or counseling is needed, the services of a competent professional should be sought.

Distributed in Canada by Raincoast Books

Copyright © 2017 by Coral Popowitz
Instant Help Books
An imprint of New Harbinger Publications, Inc.
5674 Shattuck Avenue
Oakland, CA 94609
www.newharbinger.com

Cover design by Amy Shoup

Acquired by Wendy Millstine

Edited by James Lainsbury

All Rights Reserved

Library of Congress Cataloging-in-Publication Data on file

19   18   17

10   9   8   7   6   5   4   3   2   1   First Printing

For all the grieving teens I have had the honor of meeting, knowing, and helping.

For all the teachers, mentors, funeral directors, and counselors who have listened and shown me the way.

For my family—Steve, Jess, Leo, Georgia, Mickey, Amanda, Avery, Lennon, Lainey, Selina, Alan, Elsie, Lucy, Tommy, Abe, Nicole, Lucas, Brandi, Jonah, Mariah, Johnny, Charlie, and Tiff—thank you for being twenty-three of the most amazing and patient, loving and funny, and kind and generous people with whom I get to share my laughter and tears, anger and sadness, and life and love. I count you as my greatest blessing every single day.

For Steve—the true love of my life—"more."

contents

Foreword		vii
Introduction		1
1	Your Grieving Brain	9
2	Your Grieving Body	29
3	Your Angry Body	47
4	Your Sad Body	71
5	Your Lonely Body	93
6	Your Scared Body	109
7	Your Tired Body	127
8	Your Sick Body	143
9	Your Calm Body	159
10	Your Healing Body	173
	Epilogue: Begin Again	179
	Acknowledgments	181
	Appendix A: What's Your Trauma Response?	183
	Appendix B: Depression Diagnosis Checklist	187
	Appendix C: Suicide Risk Signs	191
	References and Selected Readings	193

foreword

Life is full of change. As the author Doe Zantamata once stated:

> *If you were to open the front door and see that it had started*
> *raining, you wouldn't slam it and curse the clouds because*
> *it was sunny just an hour before. You'd get an umbrella and*
> *be on your way. Part of embracing change in life is knowing*
> *that you will be able to adapt. There is a comfort in the*
> *familiar, but new things can be better than before, or the*
> *change may even only be temporary. When faced with change*
> *that's not in your control, adapt, and be on your way.*

No matter how catastrophic a situation is, you will eventually have to accept that trying times are simply part of life. Without these hard times, you will never experience the best days of your life. As hard as it is to see in the moment, our hardships make us into more loving, grateful people who are thankful for each and every thing on this earth. Everyone will experience loss and grief at some point in their lifetime.

I always knew that without loss, there isn't life, but I never fathomed that I would personally lose someone so dear to my heart. June 5, 2013, seemed like it would be an ordinary day; I had no way of knowing that my entire life was about to get turned upside down. That was the night my family received the devastating news that my oldest sister, Kaylie—my best friend—had tragically passed away from an epileptic seizure. I was stunned and wondered how this could even be. I was supposed to be a bridesmaid in her wedding that winter. We were supposed to grow old together and be the crazy old sibling pair in the nursing home.

I quickly began to learn that grief is a roller coaster ride of a journey. The first few weeks after her death I was mostly all right, still in shock from the horrific event that happened. Once the initial shock ended, however, I was profoundly miserable, almost to the point of not wanting to live myself. I became the glue for my family, the person who held everything together, and it forced me to mature very quickly. Nothing seemed enjoyable, even things I used to love. I didn't know where to turn or what to do with myself. No one seemed to understand me. Some of my close friends just stopped talking to me because they didn't understand my grief, and I felt awkward around those who did. I felt alone, broken, and lost.

A few months after Kaylie died, my family and I attended grief camp, which is where I met Coral. I'd been hesitant about attending grief camp; I thought I would just be sitting in a circle crying with a box of Kleenex. Little did I know that it would forever change my entire perspective on life. After camp, I realized that I needed to change my way of thinking and turn a horrible situation into one filled with positive emotion. Now I strive to do everything I can to help others and make the world a better place. When I first arrived at camp, I was greeted by Coral's bubbly, caring attitude. She's the type of person you would want to help you through your challenges. She changed my life in three short days, and for that, I am forever grateful. We have remained in touch since camp, and I am proud to call her both my mentor and one of my closest friends.

Coral's knowledge and expertise on the field of grief and teens is amazing, and I can assure you that she and her book will change your life. I wish that there had been a resource like this book available after I lost Kaylie. I remember searching for books and information about grief for teens and only being able to find picture books for kids and some books for adults. This made me feel even more alone than I already did. So, when Coral mentioned that she was planning on writing a book about grief for teens, I was ecstatic. It was absolutely my honor to assist Coral with her book, providing ideas and even feedback throughout her writing process.

While reading through Coral's rough drafts, I instantly wished that I had known some of the coping strategies mentioned throughout the book during my darkest hours. I tried some of them as I read and realized how well they worked. At the time, my main coping strategy had been journaling; wonderful as it was, journaling was not able to relieve some of the anger and other intense emotions that I felt, like guilt. My sister died of a seizure alone at her apartment, but somehow I still felt guilty, like there was something I could have done to prevent it from happening. I felt like I should've been there—possibly I could even have saved her life.

Many teens experience guilt throughout the grieving process, and, if you do, there is no need to be embarrassed. It is totally normal, I can promise you. You can follow some of the exercises located in the guilt chapter and throughout the book to help relieve your grief.

Regardless of your situation, I can assure you that this book contains coping strategies that will work for you. Be warned, though, that you need to keep an open mind when trying these activities and coping strategies, because the ones that work best for you might surprise you. Throughout your grief journey, there will be bad days and good days, but it is up to you to make the most of each day. Don't be afraid to talk about your emotions with others. In fact, talking with someone reliable is really one of the best healing practices I know of.

Again, no matter your situation, I promise that you will make it through the heart-wrenching pain and grief, and this book will help, as will leaning on those around you, like your friends and loved ones. Don't be ashamed, though, if you don't see instantaneous results. The grief journey is a gradual progression with many twists and turns, ups and downs. When you lose someone you love, your life will never be the same, but you will adapt and begin to get used to the new you and your new normal. Sometimes your grief will engulf you like an ocean, and other times things will be calm. The truth is you just need to keep swimming through each and every day. It's the only way.

Thank you, Coral, for everything you have done and continue to do for me and all the other grieving children, teens, and their families. You truly have helped save many lives and turned countless others around, including mine. Love you, from the very bottom of my heart!

—Danielle Hogue

introduction

Why would I read about grief when I'm feeling it every day?

—Matt

Why does my whole body ache when my heart is broken?

—Katie

How do I deal with all that's changed? My life will never be the same.

—Emma

When someone you love has died, everything changes. The world you knew, the life you had, is different—and it will always be different. You think differently, you act differently, you feel differently, and your whole body hurts at times.

This book is about how grief not only affects your thoughts and emotions, but how it also affects your physical body. By that I mean how and why your muscles tense, why your stomach and head ache, why you're too exhausted to move, and why your body feels numb to the pain. You might sleep too much or not enough, or food may taste different; maybe you can't eat, or you overeat. You feel your heart beat faster, you can't breathe, and all these symptoms make you worry that you're going to die too.

You will be grieving a long time, maybe all your life. Grief is a journey that doesn't end, but it does change. Eventually your grief won't be as intense; it won't hurt as much or for as long or as often as it does right after someone you love has died. Understanding how and why your body reacts to grief, to the emotions and thoughts that go with it, will help you move along that grief journey. When you understand why you feel nervous, annoyed, hassled, driven, blue, or inadequate, the thoughts and feelings, the reactions your body experiences, will have less power over you (Hansen and Mendius 2009).

Knowing why and how your body reacts, however, isn't enough to move you forward. Each chapter in this book focuses on the emotions most associated with grief and how they can affect our body and our minds. Our emotions aren't separate from our bodies; in fact, they physically affect our bodies. Though the chapters discuss the different emotions that affect grief, emotions don't happen one at a time; nor do they occur in any kind of order or end once you've experienced them. When we feel grief, our minds and bodies bounce around with varying degrees of emotions, and sometimes we even feel two emotions at the same time.

Once you've read the first couple of chapters and understand the mind-body connection and how grief, loss, and trauma affect us, you can turn to the chapter that you feel is most relevant to how you feel right now. Feel free to read different chapters as your emotions change.

The whole point of this book is to introduce you to skills and activities that will help you deal with the emotions you're feeling. There are a number of ways you can help your body when emotions and thoughts around grief bubble up or overwhelm you. For example, there are activities that can help you get through class when something or someone brings up a loved one who has died. There are things you can do to help you get to sleep more quickly or manage your anger when it's out of control. Visit http://www.newharbinger.com/38532 for audio tracks, and worksheets related to the activities in this book.

Thousands of grieving teens have tested these activities. Some of them may work for you, whereas others may feel pretty weird and won't work for you. Try out the activities that you think might help you; if they do help, keep doing them. But also keep an open mind. Once in a while, try an activity that doesn't seem like it would work, or even one that seems down-right stupid. You never know what will help. You never thought you'd lose the person you love, you never thought you'd feel this much pain, and you're not sure how you're going to get through this grief, so why not try something you're not sure of and see if it helps?

The ideas and activities in this book are meant to move you closer to being in control of the anxiety, irritability, nervous-ness, depression, and general sense of "crazy" that grief—and life in general—can stir up. They will help you on your grief journey, especially on those "grief days" that come up when you thought things were getting better, and they may also help you pass your driver's license test, deal with your first job and a crabby boss, handle a breakup, or navigate college exams.

In this book you will get to know a few teens who are going through some of the same things you are; they all had a loved one who died. People react differently when someone in their life dies. Some teens want to let people know what happened right away, looking for support from others to get them through. Others don't want anyone to know that they're grieving, not wanting the pity of others or to be known as "the girl whose dad died." In this book you'll meet Emma; her four-year-old sister Sophie died when the string of her hoodie sweatshirt got caught on the slide and strangled her as she went down. Emma lives with her older brother and parents in a small town. Her story is complicated, but it's also normal. Her experiences, feelings, and thoughts may be just like yours. However, each grief story is unique because it belongs to the individual.

You'll also meet Katie, whose mom died from breast cancer after a long, hard-fought battle. Katie lives with her twin sister, her dad, and her dad's new girlfriend. Katie's grief is totally different from her sister's even though they both experienced the same loss. You, too, have your own relationship with the person who died—your own experiences, conversations, feelings, adventures, and arguments.

And then there's Matt, who struggles with an argument he had with his best friend, JR, who took his own life. Matt lives in a big city where suicide among school-age kids is not uncommon; Matt has even considered it himself. JR's suicide shocked everyone, and Matt has never felt this bad before. Here are their stories in their own words.

> Matt: *So I get a text lighting up my phone in the middle of the night. It's JR again, so I push the "off" button, roll over, and say to myself, Later, dude, it's the middle of the night.*
>
> *The next morning, I look at the message, and it says, "Ready for a wild ride?"*
>
> *Didn't know what that meant until I got to school and everyone knew but me. JR took his old man's car and ran it into a tree—on purpose. The cops think he was going at least ninety miles per hour with no seat belt. Something was*

always going on with JR. He got suspended for drinking in school, he got beat up downtown at a concert, and his parents got a divorce after years of fighting it out. He broke up with his girlfriend last month. We had argued after school the day before he killed himself about him just getting over her; he said he didn't know if he could, and I told him he better. That night, he texted her and told her he couldn't—he wouldn't—live without her, and he said good-bye.

I guess he told me good-bye too, sort of.

Every day since it happened, all I do is wonder what would have happened if I had answered his text.

Katie: *When my mom was first diagnosed, we all believed—we were all told—she would survive. There are all kinds of research and drugs and help out there for women with breast cancer, now that all the walks and runs and awareness are happening. We believed the doctors.*

She got really sick whenever she had the chemotherapy treatments. She couldn't do anything, was always throwing up in the bathroom, and never came to dinner. A lot of times my twin sister, Kelly, and I had to get her away from the toilet and back into bed because she was so weak.

Seeing her that way made me sick, too, and scared.

She would rally, and we would think that she was better, that life would go back to normal, but then she'd relapse. We had to do all the mom stuff, like laundry, dishes, cooking for my dad, cleaning the bathroom, and changing her sheets. Sometimes it was easier when she was in the hospital.

The days before she died I just remember everything being quiet and hushed except for the sound of the machines around her. She moaned a lot, and her breathing was real funny.

Everyone says I should be glad I got a chance to say good-bye to her. I am glad, I guess, though I don't think anyone really should feel glad about saying good-bye to your mother for the last time.

Emma: *That day started just like every other normal day of the past fourteen years of my life, with my mom, dad, older brother, younger sister, and the baby. The baby of the family is—or was—Sophie. When I left for school, she was whining over her soggy cereal. When I got back from school, there was an ambulance in my driveway and her tiny little body was covered with a sheet while people raced to put her inside the ambulance. She died by strangulation. I still don't understand how that kind of thing happens. I know how it happened: her hoodie got caught on a screw or something, I just don't understand how it could happen to her. How could this happen to our family?*

Matt, Katie, and Emma are composites of real teens with real grief they are living with and real questions that go unanswered. They represent teens who suddenly find themselves in a world of hurt and grief they didn't see coming and don't want to have to deal with. They, like you, just want to get back to being a normal teenager. You may wonder if "normal" will ever happen again, or you may stuff down your grief, sadness, and anger in an attempt to force a normal life. But things aren't normal anymore; someone you love has died, and things will never be the same. However, knowing some of the information in this book and doing some of its activities may answer your questions.

It may seem impossible right now to think about living normally after what has happened. This book will help you find strength, laughter, love, and joy, because you can—and want to—figure out how to live with the changes, find fun again, and get to a new normal.

chapter 1

your grieving brain

Get ready for a nerd alert. Knowing about the brain and neuroscience helps us understand why we think, feel, and act the way we do.

—Emma

Emma's right on track! This chapter is all about brainy, nerd-like stuff. Although it may be hard to connect the science presented in this chapter to how you feel right now, if you stick with reading this entire chapter, you'll see things more clearly. Understanding how your brain works, especially after a sudden trauma such as the loss of a loved one, helps take away some of the confusion over what is happening with your thoughts, feelings, and behaviors. Knowing more about your brain can also bring a sense of relief, because you can see that normal brain development is playing a big part in how you're feeling and what you're doing as a result of your grief. You're not just being or feeling crazy; rather, your still-growing brain is trying to catch up with your life experiences.

We begin with the brain because it is the part of our body that gives us the ability to move, feel, and think. Our brain controls all the functions of our body, holds our memories, and determines our emotional state; our brain lets us learn what we need so we can survive and thrive.

With teens, I usually start out any discussions about grief by talking about the brain and brain development. Most don't like it much at first; the information seems too confusing or like it doesn't matter. But as Emma said, "The more I heard, the more I knew, the better I understood, the better I felt. Knowing that my brain—anyone's brain—would find it hard to cope with having someone in my life gone forever gave me a sense of being a little closer to normal."

By understanding how her brain works, Emma learned a lot about how to cope with her grief, her emotions, and the sometimes uncontrollable aches and pains she felt in her body. So let's give it a shot.

Your Three Brains from the Bottom Up

Let's first take a look at the structure of the human brain. It's really made up of three parts, or three minibrains, if you will, that work together to integrate our experiences and to keep us alive. There's the *brain stem*, which is the part of the brain that connects to the spinal cord. It's responsible for all automatic life functions, such as breathing, heart rate, and blood pressure. It keeps your body alive and moving. You were born with a completely developed brain stem.

Next to develop is the *limbic brain*, which is your brain's emotion center. It controls feelings, mood, memory, and motivation. It's also the part of the brain that feels fear and senses threat. It is partially developed when you are born and grows the most during adolescence (Siegel 2013). To understand how the limbic brain develops, consider this example: When we're babies, we cry and scream when we're hungry, being the little survivors that we are, and when our loving caregiver shows up to feed us, we learn about love and relationships. This experience grows our limbic brain. Through this process we start to remember what we need to do to get our needs met. Our memories are also stored in the limbic brain, which explains why emotions are so easily triggered when we remember or share memories of our loved one who died.

Finally, there's the *cortex*, or thinking brain, which is the biggest part of the brain. It develops throughout your life and is the part of the brain that learns the skills of language, math, decision making, planning, and organizing. As the cortex develops, both our genetics—where we get our temperament and personality—and our life experiences make us who we are. We learn to walk and talk from this part of our brain. Once we can speak, our limbic brain starts storing our memories with words and stories. This is why we can't remember much of our lives before the age of four or five: our cortex wasn't developed enough to give us the words, the language, to store memories as stories we could tell.

Your brain is like a sponge, soaking up everything adults show and tell you until you're about twelve years old. Then your brain starts getting rid of all the stuff the sponge absorbed. This process is called *pruning*: information stored in your brain that is no longer useful dies off, leaving only the important stuff. We also call this process *maturing* (Siegel 2013).

The *prefrontal cortex* (PFC) is an essential area of our brain contained within the cortex (thinking brain) that kicks into high gear, developing at its fastest rate, when we are teens. The PFC is the part of the brain that helps us make good decisions, but it isn't finished developing until we're in our midtwenties. Being risky, making poor choices, and screwing up from time to time are part of PFC development.

The limbic (emotional) brain is at an all-time active period when you're a teenager, and the PFC is working overtime to balance exploring new possibilities and your curiosity with taking risks and making mistakes. In order to live independently of your parents, you need to form your own identity, and this normal developmental need is why you prefer your friends over your family most of the time. Once your brain has fully developed, around your midtwenties, it can still change and learn new things, which is good news. No matter what happens in our lives, our brains can grow, change, and adapt to life experiences until we're well into our nineties.

Neuroscientist Dan Siegel developed this easy activity to help us understand our brains. It's a *handy* way to remember the three parts of the brain, how the brain develops from the bottom up, and how the three parts function together. All you need is your own hand!

1.1 A Handy Tool

1. Hold your hand in the air like you are going to high-five someone, then turn the palm toward you.

2. Picture your wrist and arm as your spinal cord and the palm of your hand as the brain stem.

3. Take your thumb and fold it over your palm (brain stem); your thumb represents the limbic brain, or your emotional brain. As you can see, the emotional brain directly touches the brain stem, which shows you how and why your emotions directly affect your body.

Remember, the brain stem is what controls your body functions, such as breathing.

4. Curl your four fingers around your thumb. They represent the cortex.

5. The very tips of your four fingers, part of the cortex, represent the prefrontal cortex, or PFC. The PFC touches and affects all parts of your brain: the cortex, the limbic brain, and the brain stem.

Now you have a picture of your brain's bottom-up development, starting at the bottom of your brain with your palm (brain stem); next with your thumb layered on top (the limbic, or emotional, brain); and finally, at the top and last to develop, your finger, representing the cortex. Now you can understand how the teenage brain, especially the limbic (emotional) brain, works in overdrive; it's sandwiched right in the middle of all that brain development and is affected by both the brain stem and the cortex. So imagine what happens to your brain when it is dealt an emotional whammy with the death of a loved one.

Slammed with an Emotional Whammy

When the teenage brain hears the news of a loved one's death, shock and disbelief are usually the first reactions. This happens because the cortex, the thinking part of the brain, cannot yet process the reality of the news. The limbic (emotional) part of the brain doesn't process the feelings right away either. It's the brain stem that processes the news first.

The brain stem contains the *autonomic nervous system*. Basically, this system controls the functions of our body to keep it alive when something shocks it. This larger system is broken down into two others called the sympathetic and parasympathetic systems. The *sympathetic nervous system* ignites whenever we are frightened or threatened in any way. The *parasympathetic nervous system* calms or relaxes our nervous system when the threat subsides. As you can imagine, grief kicks your sympathetic nervous system up a notch or two and leaves it there a while.

The sympathetic and parasympathetic nervous systems developed to help us recognize threats to survival, react, and then calm the brain and body back down. Most of this response takes place in a short amount of time. Imagine a caveman encountering a lion on the savannah: the sympathetic nervous system kicks in, and the caveman either runs, pulls out a weapon to fight the lion, freezes in his tracks, or faints and plays dead, hoping the lion will go away. This reaction to threat is called the fight, flight, freeze, faint response.

Fight! Flight! Freeze! Faint!

The threat to the caveman—or to you in hearing the news of your loss—can be real, or it can *feel* like it's real. Whether or not the threat to your life—your survival—is apparent, such as a lion breathing down your neck, or perceived, such as wondering how you'll live life without this person, the response—fight, flight, freeze, faint—is automatic in the brain.

Your sympathetic nervous system kicks into gear; it's the first responder to bad news. When you are overwhelmed by an experience and your sympathetic nervous system is turned on "high" or "constant," it's what is considered a trauma reaction. The trauma moves into the limbic (emotional) brain and affects two areas: the amygdala and the hippocampus.

The *amygdala* is a tiny, almond-shaped area of the limbic brain that is our fear center. The amygdala processes all threats and the fear that goes with them. It is like our own personal fire alarm, ready to go off whenever we are threatened emotionally or physically. When the amygdala senses danger, it automatically releases stress hormones that the brain stem circulates throughout your body. Your sense of smell is located in the amygdala; it literally smells danger and gets you ready to survive.

Because the amygdala is part of the limbic (emotional) center of the brain and has been our survival fire alarm since the caveman days, it reacts to cues from the environment without thinking. The cortex (thinking brain) is not online when the amygdala is fired up. It is as if you, or more accurately your brain, has flipped its lid. Try this activity for a picture of what I mean.

1.2 Flipping Your Lid!

Use your handy model of the brain from activity 1.1. Be sure to have your hand in "full brain" mode—fist with thumb inside your fingers.

1. Imagine something terrible has just happened to you. Your sympathetic nervous system detects something is wrong and lights up your amygdala (for the sake of the handy model, your amygdala is the fingernail on your thumb).

2. The amygdala's fire alarm sounds, stress surges throughout your brain and body, and the cortex (thinking brain) goes off-line. To represent this response, raise your fingers (cortex and prefrontal cortex) off your thumb, the limbic (emotional) center. Thanks to your amygdala's quick response, you have "flipped your lid."

3. There sit all your emotions—fear, sadness, anger—right out in the open, without your cortex and prefrontal cortex to help you think your way through the situation—that is, make a plan or a smart decision.

Despite its size, the amygdala is a big deal, taking your ability to think and reason off-line in a crisis—when you really need it. This reaction can cause a lot of long-term problems. Finding ways to get your parasympathetic nervous system to calm things down and reengage your cortex (thinking brain) is what most of the activities in this book are designed to do.

Alongside the amygdala is the *hippocampus*, the memory center of the brain; it takes our memories, collected from our five senses, and stores them. Within the hippocampus there are two types of memories: explicit and implicit. *Explicit memories* are those we remember and recall; we can put words and sentences together to form a story about an experience. An explicit memory uses the cortex to develop the memory, or story, and retain it. For example, you can remember the time you went fishing and Grandpa fell into the lake. *Implicit memories* are unconscious. These we remember without thinking. For example, you had to learn how to walk or ride a bike, but now that you know how to do these things, you no longer have to tell yourself how to do them—you just remember. Our bodies remember implicit memories for us.

The amygdala and the hippocampus work together when you are threatened and affect the other parts of your brain and body. One of the first things the amygdala does is send a message to your body to release stress hormones, mainly adrenaline, to get your body ramped up to protect itself. For example, while hiking you might spot a squiggly green twig on the ground. Your amygdala fires up, thinking the twig might be a threat: *snake!* This causes your brain stem to kick up your heart rate and tense your leg muscles in case you need to run, which causes you to breathe faster. Simultaneously, your hippocampus recalls (explicitly) what a snake looks like versus a squiggly green twig. It quickly relays the information to your cortex, which pulls up an explicit memory and figures out the difference: *Oh…that's a twig, not a snake.* Then your brain stem gets the message to ease up, returning your body and your brain to normal.

Fight, flight, freeze, and faint are the primary ways your brain's sympathetic nervous system responds to threats or trauma. They are your survivor instincts. Fighting, physically striking back at the threat or trauma, is one response. Then there's flight, turning and running as far away from the threat or trauma as possible. Or you might freeze. Usually this happens in a split second, when you are not sure what you're seeing. When you see the squiggly green twig and think it's a snake, you stop, hold your breath, and wait. Fear immobilizes you.

Finally, a less likely but still possible response is to faint. Animals who are preyed upon will often exhibit this response; they go limp and lose consciousness, or "play dead," and sometimes the predator will go on its way and leave them alone. The human version of fainting is zoning out. Even though you may be physically in a given space, it feels like you are somewhere else.

Our brains respond to trauma by first using this fight, flight, freeze, faint response. (Refer to appendix A in the back of the book to better understand what kind of trauma responses you may experience.) Emma found that recognizing this automatic response helped her understand why her family members had different reactions to the loss of her little sister Sophie.

> *My older brother was real angry and went "fight" all the way. My mom kind of "fled," not talking about it at all, sort of pretending it never happened. My dad just plain "froze," walking around all robot-like. And me, I think I did the "faint" thing. I just retreated to my bed and slept day after day, sort of went unconscious, hoping to wake up and have it all be a dream.*

When our brains and bodies are overwhelmed with a traumatic experience, sometimes we can get stuck in the fight, flight, freeze, faint response, feeling as though our ability to think clearly, to concentrate or make decisions, is never coming back online.

Stuck in Trauma and Grief

The autonomic nervous system is meant for those caveman reactions to a threat: response and survival (sympathetic nervous system) and back to calm (parasympathetic nervous system). Once the threat is gone, recovery should be automatic. However, we can become stuck when our bodies fill with stress hormones that aren't released and we have no way—or believe we have no way—to get our "lid" back on. When we have no way to relieve stress, to calm our feelings and allow our cortex and prefrontal cortex to do their work, we can get stuck on the emotional side of an experience. Our feelings can leave us exposed and raw, unable to comprehend how we will survive a loss.

For example, you may have a feeling of dread, worrying that someone else will suddenly die. You may have fears, as Katie did, about who would take care of you if both your parents died. You may have feelings of guilt, like Matt, wondering what you could have done to have prevented something from happening. Perhaps you're like Emma, and you want to sleep so you don't have to remember.

On top of all these feelings you also have the normal teenage emotions and experiences, such as anxiety about getting your homework in on time or achieving decent grades in chemistry so you can get into college. You worry about your best friend not texting you back and whether or not you'll get asked to the prom. And it feels like none of those things matter at all now that someone you love has died. Up and down your emotions go, each and every day, stuck on a roller coaster ride you want to get off. Emma describes being stuck in grief and trauma this way:

> Your grieving brain keeps churning away, spinning out of control like a feather in the wind. Your brain is a heavy, wet towel, and nothing is sinking in, nothing matters. Every day it feels like your brain is overloaded or on fire; you're too tired or too angry or too sad to function, and you're angry and sad and tired of what's happening to you. You ask yourself, Will it get better? When will it get better? If it gets better, does that mean I forget? How will I live the rest of my life like this? Why did this happen to me? Or to my loved one? Will I ever be normal again?

Emma was stuck in her grief and emotions, with questions being asked over and over again in her brain. There are ways to move away from the brain's sympathetic nervous system responses (flipped lid) and get the parasympathetic nervous system (calm mind and body) back. You can get off the roller coaster of emotions for small periods of time in order to let your brain calm down, to cease the amygdala's alarm, and to bring your whole brain back online. First things first: pause and take a breath. Doing so will help remove some of the stress that has built up in your body.

1.3 Pause to Breathe!

Stop what you're doing and what you're thinking or feeling. Whatever is happening, pause and just breathe. If you want, for this activity, set your phone alarm for five minutes.

1. Pay attention to your breathing right now. Is it fast, shallow, slow, or normal? Are you sighing?

2. Put one hand on your stomach at your belly button and the other on your chest just below the base of your neck. Keep breathing, feeling your breath move in and out of your body.

3. With the next breath, imagine you are going to blow up a balloon in your belly. Feel your hand move up as you fill every part of your lungs with oxygen. You may feel like you can't push any more air into your lungs.

4. Next, slowly, with control, release your breath—the air out of the balloon—until your belly button feels like it's touching your backbone. Open your mouth a little, blowing the air out of your body as if you are slowly blowing out the candles on a birthday cake.

5. Do at least three of these deep balloon-belly breaths.

Deep belly breathing like this can do amazing things for your grieving brain. If you are feeling nervous or anxious, pause and take three deep belly breaths and see if things change. After you've finished a good, long cry, remember to take three deep belly breaths to restore the oxygen to your brain. When you're having trouble falling asleep, try to get through twenty deep belly breaths; you'll probably be asleep long before you get all twenty in.

1.4 Square Breathing

A variation of deep belly breathing is square breathing. This technique will help take your mind off all your worries or fears and help you concentrate on the present moment (Santa Clara University Cowell Center n.d.).

1. As you breathe in deeply, filling your lungs, count to four slowly.

2. Next, hold your breath and count to four.

3. Slowly breathe out, counting to four.

4. Now, hold your breath to the count of four—and begin again.

5. Do six "square" rounds when you are feeling overwhelmed with any emotion.

It seems kind of silly to have techniques for breathing, because breathing is an automatic brain stem activity already. We breathe all day every day, without working at it. From our very first breath until our last, our brain stem makes sure we breathe so our body gets the oxygen it needs to live and grow. In addition to breathing *in* oxygen, it's just as important that we breathe *out*. We need to release the buildup of carbon dioxide in our bodies to stay healthy.

The reason deep breathing is different from normal breathing is that when our bodies are stressed, our brain and our sympathetic nervous system alter our breathing to meet the demands. When we run, our breathing changes; it speeds up, and we take in small, quick gulps of oxygen. When we run too far too fast, we find ourselves gasping for breath. When we are afraid, we may hold our breath, denying our body of needed oxygen, and then let out a huge sigh, pushing too much carbon dioxide out of our body, which can lead to hyperventilation or fainting. When we cry from emotional pain, we may have short, sobbing breaths or feel like we can't catch our breath because we're crying so hard. Deep breathing can help replenish the oxygen lost from stressed breathing and remove the buildup of carbon dioxide that can cause shortness of breath, fatigue, headaches, sleepiness, confusion, and a host of other symptoms that keep the body and brain off balance.

Mind Full of Grief

Another way to restore balance to your body and brain with breathing is to practice mindfulness. *Mindfulness* is about checking in with yourself, being where you are right now, in this moment. It's letting your thoughts and feelings about the past or the future slide on by like clouds in the sky. Or you could see these thoughts and feelings as little thought bubbles that float away or burst. Mindfulness is a remote control you can use to pause your scattered thoughts and intense feelings for just a minute or two—or maybe ten minutes. Mindfulness purposely lets your mind know that you are in control and can guide it—not the other way around!

Researchers have proven (Flaxman and Flook n.d.) that mindfulness can improve your attention and memory (for test taking), social relationships (including family relationships), ability to tolerate pain (emotional and physical), and immune system (so you get sick less often).

Most importantly for a developing teenage brain, mindfulness shrinks the amygdala, reducing the stress response, especially feelings of fear. Mindfulness also thickens the prefrontal cortex so you can think more clearly, make better decisions, have better judgment, and better plan and organize life (Lazar et al. 2005). Give it a try.

1.5 Mindful Minutes

Find a private spot—in your room, outdoors—where you feel safe and comfortable and will have few distractions. Set your phone timer or alarm clock for three minutes, making sure it's far enough away that it won't startle you when it goes off. (You can download the audio version of this activity at http://www.newharbinger.com/38532.)

1. Sit comfortably with your feet flat on the ground and your hands in your lap, or lie down on a rug or towel placed on the floor with your arms by your side, palms up. (Lying on your bed may cause you to fall asleep.)

2. Close your eyes or lower your gaze so you are not distracted by the things around you. Keep the room quiet, or play music without lyrics on low volume. Take a few minutes to just breathe and adapt to this activity.

3. Take one or two square breaths (activity 1.4), and feel your body relax.

4. Now breathe regularly. Pay attention; be mindful of your breath going in your body naturally, and then notice your breath leaving your body. Notice how your chest rises and falls, and hear the sounds of your breath.

5. Don't control your breath; let your parasympathetic nervous system do its work of naturally calming you down, letting you breathe automatically and implicitly, without having to think about it. Just breathe.

6. As thoughts pop into your mind—*Am I doing this right? This is dumb! What's supposed to be happening? What if someone sees me?*—just let each one of them go. Think of them as floating clouds or thought bubbles passing through, in and out of your mind.

7. Feelings may also come up: sadness, boredom, silliness, anger. Don't react to the feeling, just notice it and see how it passes with the next breath or two and turns into something else—a different thought, a different feeling.

8. Continue to practice letting your thoughts and feelings go, coming back each time to concentrate on your breath. Keep following the in and out of your breath until the alarm goes off. Once it has, take one more deep breath and end your mindfulness practice. That's it. Simple, but not easy.

If three minutes feels too uncomfortable, start with one minute. Once three minutes seems to go by quickly, set the alarm for five minutes. Keep practicing and increasing your time; ten minutes a day is great, and twenty minutes is ideal.

Beyond all the good results of mindfulness research, the most important reason to practice mindfulness while grieving

is so you can be in the present moment, in the right now. So much about grief and grieving is about sadness in the past, all the woulda, coulda, shouldas; the memories; the what-ifs and how comes. Grief often brings anxiety and worry about the future. What's going to happen now? Who will walk me down the aisle or teach me to drive? Will we be poor now that Dad's not here? Can I still leave home for college feeling this way? Practicing mindfulness allows you to set aside the past and the future and just *be* in the present moment.

Remember, it's called mindfulness *practice* because you don't get perfect at it, and you won't remember to do it every day. On some days the bubbles burst, and on others they just pester you the whole time. Regardless, just keep practicing, trying mindfulness again and again. The more you practice, the more you will be able to recognize and notice what is happening in your mind, in your body, and in the world around you.

On some days, especially grief days or days when you don't want to think about or notice anything, you may just want a break from it all. That's okay; just rest everything in your brain. Have some mindless moments.

1.6 Mindless Moments

The preparation for mindless moments varies according to the activity you choose.

1. Watching silly no-brainer movies.

2. Binge-watch television shows from the seventies or eighties on Netflix.

3. Color in a coloring book with new crayons.

4. Put together a one-thousand-piece puzzle.

5. Doodle.

6. Play classic video games such as Super Mario, Pac-Man, or Pong.

7. Walk the dog.

8. Ride your bike.

9. Stare at the clouds and look for animal shapes.

10. Hang out with someone under the age of five or over seventy-five.

11. Do your laundry.

12. Learn to juggle.

13. Deep clean your room.

14. Bounce a ball.

15. Float in a lake, a pool, or the tub.

There are many ways to give your grieving brain a rest and just be in the moment without doing or thinking about anything. By slowing down mental activity, returning to activities that are part of your implicit memory and require little effort, you can reduce stress and relax.

When we occasionally give our brain a mental break, we give it the energy it needs to keep growing and developing. Just like we need sleep and food and water, we need mental relaxation to function in a healthy way. You can't, however, be in that mindless, relaxed state too often or stay in it too long. You need to reconnect with your brain and get it back online and back to everyday living. Practicing mindfulness will help you get back online. Emma has some great suggestions for how to deal with mindless and mindful practices:

> *Be sure to make time to do both practices, and don't forget to use your phone alarm or something else to keep track of how long you practice. If you don't notice when you need to stop mindless moments, some adult is going to let you know, believe me. Better to figure out how much time you're going to spend on this activity and stick to it; it's easy to get lost in this one.*

> *Practicing mindfulness is hard, and setting a time limit helps a lot. After all, you can do just about anything if you know how long it will last. Those thoughts and feelings that pop up are tough to deal with. Eventually, the thoughts and feelings I had weren't always about Sophie, or my grief. By doing mindfulness, I found that my thoughts and feelings don't last forever; they may hang around for a while, and they may pop up, but they don't have to take over. Mindfulness helped me notice my feelings and thoughts and practice letting them go. Grief is that way too, a practice of letting go.*

Wrap-Up

Knowing how trauma affects your brain and body and which trauma response you are experiencing may help explain why you're getting into arguments or fights, having nightmares and zoning out, or struggling to concentrate on schoolwork because you can't remember what you just read. Your teenage brain wants to stay focused on being with your friends and living your own life, whereas your family wants you closer to them. Your grieving brain feels like your family just doesn't get it, and sometimes it thinks that your friends don't get it either. During all this, your amygdala and hippocampus make you want to run away from everything that reminds you of loss—a song, a smell, a photograph—and can bring you right back to your grief. You feel torn; you want the pain to end, but you don't want to forget what happened. You don't want to be "the girl whose mom died" or "that boy whose friend killed himself." You just want to be you again.

Taking time to breathe deeply, practice mindfulness, or rest in mindless activities can help your stressed-out brain calm down. These practices can help you get over the grief and get back to a normal life. The next chapter will take a look at your whole body, what triggers it, and what will help it rest and relax when feelings and memories become overwhelming.

What's Next?

In the next chapter we'll learn more about how the body gets triggered in trauma and grief, what it means to be embodied, and what our senses have to do with all of this. Getting to the heart of the matter and finding balance in the body will relieve the physical aches and pains that may have popped up during grief.

chapter 2

your grieving body

My brain hurt, my heart hurt, my eyes hurt, my stomach hurt,
my whole body hurt—everywhere hurt.

—Emma

Imagine for a minute that you just heard a loud noise in the room—sudden, unexpected, and possibly dangerous. You know what happens in your brain, because in chapter 1 we looked at how the brain develops and responds to trauma. The sympathetic nervous system in the brain stem alerts the limbic (emotional) brain with a fight, flight, freeze, faint signal and sends all kinds of signals to your body about how to respond. This chapter is about how your body responds once your brain sends out the alarm that something is potentially dangerous or threatening.

The Body Under Stress

What does your body do when you unexpectedly hear a loud noise? First it startles, a natural reflex that may take the form of a quick gasp of air, ducking down, or turning your head quickly in the direction of the noise. This reflex, when your body automatically reacts to a stressful situation without thinking, is known as a *stress response*. The lower areas of your brain are activated during this response, but the cortex is not yet dealing with the stimulus. In other words, you've "flipped your lid" when your stress response kicks in.

After the stress response, the cortex—where your thoughts and explicit memories are housed—figures out what the loud noise was. In this example, let's say it was just a firecracker outside. It's the Fourth of July, you realize, and what you heard is a natural noise for this time of year. Now your parasympathetic nervous system takes over and begins to calm your body; you take a long, deep breath or sigh because you realize you are not in danger. You might shake your head a little at how silly you were to jump like that over a firecracker and then go about doing whatever you were doing before the noise. In the meantime, your body is working hard to lower your heart rate; return your breathing to normal; absorb the overload of stress hormones your brain produced in the nanosecond that followed the noise; and return your body to its normal, balanced level of functioning.

What happens if you are living with—and surviving—the death of someone you love and your brain and body are stressed over and over every day? You are living in a state of *chronic stress response*. Your brain keeps trying to absorb the shock and the "threat" to your day-to-day normal living. Your sympathetic nervous system is activated and continues to pump your body full of stress hormones, waiting for the cortex to understand and accept the reality of your new normal. Chronic stress response is similar to being stuck in trauma, as discussed in chapter 1; your stuck brain keeps generating stress hormones and keeps the amygdala on alert, sending adrenaline throughout your body. *Your body is not meant to be in a chronic state of threat.*

The chronic stress response can cause symptoms throughout your body, including tiredness and lack of energy; a short temper and anger; headaches and migraines; muscle stiffness and tension; stomachaches and nausea; increased acne, hair loss, and chest pains; difficulty breathing; fast heart rates; and pain or stiffness in the joints (American Psychological Association 2016). Chronic stress over the long term can lead to heart disease, diabetes, and strokes, mostly in adults, but more and more cases of adolescent heart failure and juvenile diabetes are being reported (Felitti et al. 1998). The human body is designed to survive, but it was not built to endure chronic stress. Our earliest ancestors had to survive lions and tigers and woolly mammoths every day, but they only lived twenty or thirty years. Whether you are in danger or not, the body initially responds the same way. This book and its activities will help you calm your body, either right away or once the danger is no longer present.

The body is its healthiest and strongest, with the best immune system, during adolescence (Siegel 2013). However, when exposed to chronic stress, such as the stress of grieving, the body—even the adolescent body—responds by feeling pain, getting sick, and being tired.

How your body responds to grief, how your mind tries to understand it, and the feelings you have around it are unique to you and you alone. Take a minute and look at your thumb-print. You are the only person with this thumbprint; there are more than fourteen billion thumbprints among the seven billion people in the world, but none are exactly like yours. Your body is also different from the seven billion other bodies on the planet, as is your grief. Your experiences and memories are different from even those people to whom you are closest, including siblings and parents.

It's important to pay attention to what is happening in your body when you're under stress. We sometimes get lost in our emotions or our thoughts about what's going on and forget to pay attention to how our body is dealing with the experience. It's important to be *embodied*, which means you are in your body, are aware of what is happening to it, and are able to feel sensations and emotions in it. Being embodied makes you a healthy human being and can heal your body when it hurts. Test out how embodied you are with the following activity.

2.1 What's Going On?

Find a calm place where you can sit for five minutes without distraction. Get still and quiet (activity 1.3, pause to breathe) and be mindful (activity 1.5, mindful minutes).

1. Focus your attention on your head. Notice whether there is pain, numbness, heat, or cold. If there's pain, where is it located? Across your forehead, near your neck, at your temples, in your jaw? How would you rate the pain on a scale of one to ten (one being very mild and ten being intense)?

2. Focus on your eyes. Are they strained and sore? What about your ears? Your nose and mouth? Notice any sensations or feelings

and describe them to yourself. You don't have to find the pain; just notice if there is any or what the feeling or sensation is.

3. Then move on to your neck and shoulders. Are they tense or relaxed? Is there pain? Now consider your chest. What's happening there with your breathing and heart?

4. Move down your arms, hands, and fingers. Do you notice anything here?

5. Focus next on your stomach. Any aches or pains? Rate them from one to ten.

6. Now move on to your pelvis and hips, upper legs, lower legs, and feet. One by one, notice each area of your body. You don't need to look for pain; just notice what your body feels like in this moment.

By paying attention and noticing your body, you are connecting to it. Your body is not just a thing you carry your brain and heart around in. Your body is the container for all of who you are—your thoughts, feelings, aches, pains, memories, and ideas. Noticing how your body is doing; what it feels like; and whether it is warm or cold, relaxed or tense, hungry or tired, painful or comfortable is important to your health, your healing, and your emotional well-being. Being embodied will help you get through your grief and move forward with the rest of your life.

Once you are able to notice the physical sensations in your body, you will be able to determine what pain subsides and what pain is steady or extreme. Continue to practice activity 2.1 above, and take notes each time. If you are experiencing extreme pain in one area of your body, ask to see a doctor.

Emma kept notes and brought them to her doctor and therapist appointments. She knew what her body was feeling; she knew something was going on, even if her doctor didn't.

I kept having these pains in my legs, and they were intense; I felt like I couldn't move a muscle without feeling a knife stabbing me. The pain kept me home from school a lot of days. Of course my mom took me to the doctor and I had all kinds of tests, but nothing showed up. After a while it was hard for people to believe I was in pain, but I really was!

With the help of a therapist, and because Emma understood how the body holds memories and emotions that can lead to physical pain, Emma was able to find the source of her pain.

Your Body Memory

Body memory is your implicit memory; it comprises the sensations, movements, and autonomic (occurring involuntarily) processes unique to you. Body memory can bring forth a lot of physical pain during grieving. Moms who lose babies talk about feeling physical pain in their arms, where they used to hold their baby. Widows or widowers can physically feel their hearts break when the person they loved for decades dies. Known as *broken heart syndrome* or *stress cardiomyopathy*, the stress of losing one's spouse can quickly and severely weaken actual heart muscle (Johns Hopkins Medicine n.d.). These experiences prove that grief affects our bodies, not just our feelings and thoughts.

When your body is in pain and your heart is broken, it may seem to make more sense to just avoid thinking about your loved one altogether. It may seem easier to stuff your pain deep down inside and deny that you feel anything. When you're sitting in class, it may seem like you have to keep your feelings all in, avoid them, and pretend they're not there in order to get through the day.

Understanding body memory shows you that you can't think your way through grief. You can't hide from it or tell yourself to get over it. Your body goes through grief whether you want it to or not. As Emma's experience with leg pain shows us, it can be hard to connect physical pain in the body with feelings of grief.

My therapist helped me understand how the pain in my legs was my body's way of staying in bed, immobile, and away from everything that reminded me of Sophie. It was also my way of stuffing my grief way down in my legs.

Stuffing Grief

Grief hurts. It can feel like it takes over your life, and eventually you get sick of being sad or feel angry that you are grieving. Sometimes it feels a lot easier and better to just forget about it and stuff it down, ignore it, and avoid it altogether—the feelings, the memories, the thoughts. If only it were that easy.

Studies have shown that if you suppress, deny, hide, or set aside your grief and tell yourself it isn't there or doesn't matter, your body will tell you otherwise (Van Middendorp et al. 2008). Many people want to avoid grief or delay it. Skipping the grief reactions during the school day is not a bad thing. In fact, doing so may be a necessary part of how you heal from your grief and serve as a great way to cope. It is the attempt to avoid grief completely, to not express or respond at all to your feelings and memories around the loss of the person you loved, that will worsen your situation in the long run.

Stuffing or denying your grief, keeping intense feelings, especially of anger or guilt, inside your body can cause a host of long-term physical effects. Think of the grief you push down as a loud noise you have to keep quieting; doing so stresses your body (Crenshaw 2007). Like a festering sore, the grief will come up when you least expect it. This is called *distorted grief*, an intense grief reaction that can appear years later when you're at the movie theater with your friends in college; something on the screen may make you scream out, or tears may roll down your cheeks uncontrollably. Distorted grief often appears when someone less significant in your life dies and your reaction is over the top, to the surprise of you and everyone who knows you.

Allowing yourself to experience the pain of loss, to find comfort in yourself and in others, will get you and your body through grief. Remember, the parasympathetic nervous system in your brain runs throughout your body and is ready to calm you naturally. One way to use the natural rhythms of your body to calm down is to imitate the steady beat of your own heart.

2.2 Your Beating Heart

The preparation varies depending on which activity below you choose. Each one will help you calm your body, bringing it needed balance with the implicit body memory of the rhythm of a steady, unstressed heartbeat.

- Rock back and forth and side to side. Rocking is not just for grandmothers and crying babies. It may revive implicit memories of being comforted and soothed as a baby. The rocking rhythm can calm anxiety, even if you start off rocking fast; eventually your body's relaxation response kicks in and slows the pace.

- Bounce slowly and rhythmically up and down while seated on a big yoga ball. Bounce on your backyard trampoline with a slow, steady rhythm.

- Jump rope with a steady rhythm; it has the effect of restoring the natural rhythm of your heartbeat, and it is good exercise.

- Tap your knees or the tops of your hands, or tap your feet in a slow rhythm, one side at a time. It helps your brain adapt to stress and get back its normal, slow, steady, relaxed state rather than the fast, unpredictable state of stress (Leeds 2009).

- Cross your arms, and with your palms facing you, hook your thumbs together and lay your palms on your chest at your collarbone. Slowly, as if a butterfly has landed on your chest, lift the fingers of one hand and tap them down; then lift the fingers of the other hand and tap them down. Alternate each hand back and forth in a slow, steady rhythm. This is called butterfly wings (Leeds 2009).

Your body also holds memories through your senses. We start out life with a very strong sense of smell. This sense is directly connected to the hippocampus, where memories are stored in our limbic (emotional) brain. Smells are our primary way of checking out the world, and most of our stored memories are based on smell.

Like the sense of smell, hearing, seeing, tasting, and feeling are also with us when we draw our first breath. They all are the mechanisms—the portals, so to speak—through which we make sense of the world. Our senses are strongest early in life, giving us body memories, or sense memories, which we remember implicitly for the rest of our lives. Once our cortex (thinking brain) has developed language and explicit memory, we make connections between memories and emotions and our senses. For example, a familiar smell will remind us of Grandma's cookies, and a particular song on the radio will remind us of a certain time at the beach. Understanding how our senses connect with emotions and memories helps us during stressful times. We can recognize what triggered a strong emotion or what might calm us.

When we are stressed and threatened, it is our senses that pay attention first. What we smell, see, hear, feel, or taste alerts us to danger before our thoughts can understand what is happening. The following activities are meant to heighten your senses so you can use them to restore calm to your life.

2.3 Making Sense

To better understand what is going on in your body and how senses trigger stressful or calming reactions with each of the following sense experiences, it's helpful to keep a notebook handy to describe what happens.

What's That Smell?

1. Be still (activity 1.3, pause to breathe), and try to recall different smells or scents that you connect to a particular memory. The smell of chocolate chip cookies or a fresh loaf of cinnamon bread may conjure up memories of baking with your grandmother or waking up on cold winter mornings anxious to have breakfast with the

family. The aftershave your grandfather doused himself with or the smell of seawater may remind you of going to the beach as a kid.

2. Make a list of smells and the memories they connect to. It will probably take several days or weeks to really feel like you have a good "scents" list.

3. Notice how your body feels when you recall these smells and the memories attached to them. Do they soothe you or trigger a painful feeling? Where is the pain located in your body? If you are soothed, what does that feel like in your body?

4. Certain smells can calm people or relieve stress. Lavender and rosemary, in particular, help calm strong emotions (Gedney, Glover, and Fillingim 2004). You can purchase essential oils of these scents at a health food store.

5. Place a drop or two on a cotton ball or swab and apply it to your wrist, behind your ear, or on your chest. The smell can relieve stress and provide relaxation.

6. If the essential oil of lavender or rosemary is helpful, you can also place a few drops on your pillow at night to help you sleep, or put a few drops in unscented lotion and massage it into your hands or rub it on your face.

If certain smells trigger a memory that is stressful, having worked through this activity to identify what they are can help ease your reaction when the smells come up again. Knowing ahead of time how a memory is connected to a particular smell, such as the perfume that your mother always wore, can make the scent feel less shocking, and using calming scents (with deep breathing) can relieve your body of the stress these sense memories bring about.

My Grief Playlist

1. Put together your own playlist of songs that soothe and comfort you. Your list can include songs that help you remember good times you shared with a loved one. If there's a song that seems to describe exactly how you feel, add it to your playlist. You can also add songs that let you have a good cry, releasing your sadness. If you are stumped for ideas, check out the list of songs at this web page: http://www.whatsyourgrief.com/100-songs -about-grief-and-loss.

2. Use your playlist to fall asleep, while moving your body (activity 4.1, move), or when you're doing nothing but relaxing (activity 1.6, mind-less moments). You can create multiple playlists according to your needs. Your "sleep" playlist and your "move!" playlist will probably be very different. Maybe you have a playlist "to remember" and one "to forget."

3. When you're ready, share your playlist with someone else. This is a great way to let the person know how you're feeling and to get some ideas for other songs that might be helpful.

Katie made "remember her" and "forget the pain" playlists. They really helped her the first year, when her grief was fresh and she still couldn't believe her mom had died.

Pet the Dog

In terms of your sense of touch and restoring the natural rhythm of your body (activity 2.2, your beating heart), this activity works best if you have a pet or access to a pet. If you don't, any smooth material or fabric will work, or you can dig out your old teddy bear. You can also buy yourself a new stuffed animal if need be; no one needs to know it's for you.

1. Intentionally set aside time to pet your dog, cat, gerbil, hamster, horse, or parrot. About the only pet you can't use for this activity is a fish.

2. Hold your pet, and using long, slow, rhythmic strokes, softly and mindfully (activity 1.5, mindful minutes) pet one side of your pet's body and then the other. Pay attention to how the fur, skin, or feathers feel. Notice how relaxed your pet becomes, how its body moves and molds to the stroke of your hand. Do this quietly or listen to music (perhaps your grief playlist).

3. Practice this regularly to soothe, comfort, and relax your body to reduce its stress.

Pets bring so much to our emotional world and our mental, emotional, and physical healing (Cherniack and Cherniack 2014). Remember, a pet's nature is to love you unconditionally, which you witness when your dog greets you with barking, tail wagging, and jumping-up-and-down excitement every single time you come home! This behavior in and of itself is comforting—mentally, physically, and emotionally. Also, a pet is a wonderful being to confide in; it can hear all your secrets and guarantee that it won't repeat them to anyone.

Savor the Sweetness

You'll need to find a sweet morsel of wrapped-up food, such as a piece of candy that has a wrapper or fruit that needs peeling. For the purposes of this activity, we'll imagine a small piece of chocolate. (You can download the audio version of this activity at http://www.newharbinger.com/38532.)

1. Take a couple of deep breaths.

2. Place the chocolate on the palm of your hand and bring it up to eye level. Look at it; study it for just a bit. Notice the pretty silver wrapper

and the size and shape of the chocolate. Think for a minute about what it took to make this little morsel of chocolate. Who thought of it? Where did it get its name? Give yourself time to enjoy the moment and savor some of the qualities of this sweet treat.

3. Keeping the chocolate at eye level in your palm, slowly begin to unwrap it, unfolding the wrapper all the way around the chocolate. Take your time, peeling it away as slowly as you can. Be intentional about taking your time.

4. Now look at what's in your hand, the shape, the size. You can probably smell the chocolate now, and maybe you can feel your mouth starting to water as your taste buds trigger a reaction.

5. Place the chocolate on your tongue and let it sit there a second or two before you close your mouth. Don't bite down; rather, let the chocolate sit, melting and covering your whole tongue and all its taste buds.

6. As the chocolate is melting and you are savoring its flavor, think about some of the sweet moments in your life, the ones that seemed to go on forever, or at least those you wanted to go on forever. Recall some of the memories of your loved one that make you laugh or smile or give you a feeling of pride or true love for that person. Savor the past moments.

7. Still letting the chocolate melt in your mouth, think of the moments since your loved one died, moments when a friend said or did just the right thing, times when your family shared a memory and everyone smiled or laughed. Savor the sweetness of those present moments as you savor the taste of chocolate slowly melting away.

This activity is bittersweet. Sometimes it's bitter to remember what is gone, knowing that moments melt away just like the chocolate in your mouth, and you don't get them back. And it's sweet because when we pay attention, when we notice the sweetness, it lingers, and we remember better and get to enjoy it more.

Our memories may be full of this bittersweet taste popping up in our heads when we don't expect it. Yet, now that we have this experience of losing a loved one and having just memories, we can find ourselves savoring the sweetness of not just our memories but of the life we're living.

Imagination Creations

Collect magazines, newspapers, or anything with images that catch your eye. Or have your smartphone handy to take pictures of your environment.

1. Spend about an hour a week searching for images; try to get five or six.

2. Sort through the images and set aside one or two each week that you have a connection to, that you "feel in your gut" or that move your imagination beyond the image shown. Look for a theme or a purpose to the images you have collected. How are they similar and different?

3. Think about images that portray your grief or any of your emotions. Look for images that remind you of the person who died or are of things you would share with this person if you could. Find images that show this person's favorite color or thing.

4. Do this for six to eight weeks, or until you have ten to twelve images that have meaning for you, capture your feelings, make you curious, and help you dream. What do the images say about you? Do they describe your experience? How do you see these images helping you?

5. Now create a collage or a poster with the images to hang on your wall, or put them in a book or decorate a box with them. Add words or quotes to the images if you want.

6. Keep your creation out for others to see and talk about, or share it with one person you trust.

Emma noticed that she was collecting a lot of images of playgrounds and ones that represented anger. She hadn't realized that she was angry about the loss of her sister; she mostly felt sad, but she perceived her own anger after creating a collage of images glued onto cardboard. She then burned the collage in a backyard campfire. Seeing the images burn away, feeling the anger, and perceiving the release of anger as the images went up in smoke helped her heal.

Wrap-Up

Knowing how your body responds to stress, noticing what you are feeling in your body, finding ways to relax and restore the rhythm of your body, and heightening your senses can all restore balance to your body and life. The upcoming chapters will begin looking at the emotions that typically accompany grief, how our bodies react to those emotions, and what we can do to heal our grieving body. We'll start with a big emotion—anger—in the next chapter.

What's Next?

At first it's confusing to feel angry instead of sad about losing a loved one. Until we begin to think about how unfair it is—until we find something or someone to blame or be mad at for how much our life has changed. Sometimes being mad is just easier and more familiar. Chapter 3 will help you understand how anger feels in the body, what sets anger off, and what to do to relieve some of the anger without getting into trouble!

chapter 3

your angry body

*Sometimes the anger, the rage at how unfair this is, takes over…
and then you lose it—because you have to get rid of the tightness
in your muscles, the burning in your eyes, your heart beating so
fast you think it might explode.*

—Matt

*My brother got all kinds of mad and was always throwing stuff
around, screaming and yelling, making everyone nervous and
scared—especially my parents. I hated him for doing that to
our family.*

—Emma

Losing someone you love is unfair, and that is a fair reason to
feel angry. Whether the death is sudden and unexpected or
drags on because of cancer or Alzheimer's disease, it can cause
the traumatic stress response of fight and the automatic bodily
responses that go with it.

Anger is often the first emotion we feel when someone we
love dies. It's a normal feeling, especially at first, though it may

surprise us because we expect to be sad when someone dies, not mad. We don't want to believe what has happened; we don't want it to be true. We want to know why or how our loved one died or who caused the death. We can't fix it or control it; it's so unfair, and we so badly want this person back in our life.

Depending on our culture, our gender, our personality, or our family rules, expressing anger can be confusing. Often girls are expected to suppress their anger, whereas boys can express it a little—and at least for some boys, doing so seems more acceptable than showing sadness. Whether this is your first experience with the death of a loved one and you've never felt this way before, or you've had multiple losses in your life and you just can't take it anymore, you may not know what to do with your anger. Whether you express or suppress your anger, your body responds to it with:

a. tension in all your big muscle groups, especially your legs, though smaller muscles, such as those of your mouth and jaw, tighten too;

b. increased blood flow to your heart so it can pump needed blood and oxygen throughout your body, which is why your face becomes red and feels like it's burning when you're angry;

c. shallow and rapid breathing; and

d. stomachaches and headaches due to the decreased blood flow and lack of oxygen to these areas.

Here is an activity to help you relax and release the stress energy that anger produces in your body.

3.1 Whole Body Muscle Relaxation

After you've noticed or felt the fight response in your body, if you can, lie down on your back on the carpet or a rug on the floor. Don't try this activity in your bed; it's too easy to fall asleep while doing it. You can also sit in a comfortable chair or even your desk at school. (You can download the audio version of this activity at http://www.newharbinger.com/38532.)

1. Start by taking three deep breaths. You don't want to sigh or gulp air; rather, keep the breaths slow and deep to counteract the shallow, fast breath of the anger response. As you breathe in, count slowly to four while you focus on your belly moving out—like you're blowing up a balloon in your belly. Fill your whole chest with the breath. Next, exhale the breath, imagining your belly button pushing against your backbone, while slowly counting to eight. Yes, exhale twice as long as you inhale. This pushes all the carbon dioxide out of your lungs and allows your body's natural calming response—the opposite of fight, flight, freeze, faint—to take charge and slow down your heart rate and breathing and lower your blood pressure. Slowing down that rapid, shallow breathing that comes with anger will provide your brain with more oxygen, allowing you to concentrate and think clearly.

2. Now we are going to progressively relax all the muscles in your body, calming down the stress response, releasing the anger energy, and getting your brain and body back to normal. Begin by focusing on your feet; tighten the muscles in your feet like you are trying to pick up a Ping-Pong ball with your toes. Squeeze the toes tight while counting to four. Then release, letting the Ping-Pong ball drop, and take a deep breath. Do this a couple of times to get a feel for it.

3. Next, tighten your legs like you are riding a bucking horse. Hold on tight to the count of four and release, taking a deep breath. Repeat two more times.

4. Now squeeze all the muscles of your pelvis tight like you have to go to the bathroom and it's two blocks away! Hold tight and release, taking a deep breath. Try it a couple more times.

5. Now focus on your stomach. Squeeze it in like there is an orange resting on it and you want to fold it into your belly. Hold the orange tightly while you count to four. Let the muscles relax, and take another deep breath. Repeat twice.

6. Move to your chest and tighten the muscles around your heart as if an elephant is stepping on it. Count to four and release, taking a deep breath. Do this two more times.

7. Next, lift your shoulders up to your ears in a huge shrug, count to four, and release, taking a breath. Do this twice more.

8. Imagine there is a lemon in each of your hands and squeeze them as hard as you can. Let the lemons burst open if they need to— they're imaginary, after all! Then release and take a breath. Squeeze the lemons two more times.

9. Move your attention up to your head and face. Imagine biting down on a small stick as you clench your jaw, counting to four and releasing with a deep breath. Now pretend there's a fly on your nose; squeeze your lips, move your mouth, and crinkle your nose as you try to shoo the fly while counting to four. When it's gone, you can take a deep breath. Imagine that the lemon juice you squeezed with your hands just squirted into your eyes. Close them tightly while you count to four, then open them while you take another deep breath. Finally, raise your eyebrows high enough to touch your hairline, then let them relax. Do all these exercises two more times. Finish with three long, slow, deep breaths.

With this activity, you can imagine anything you'd like in order to get each of your muscle groups to tighten as you slowly move from your toes to your head, or you can move from your head to your toes. It doesn't matter; as long as you tighten and release all the muscles in your body, you're doing what's important. Like anything new and different, this activity may feel weird and uncomfortable at first. Go ahead and laugh during any of it; it doesn't have to be serious. Maybe the joke about squeezing your pelvis like the bathroom is two blocks away grosses you out. Feel free to change it up; use your imagination or sense of humor to picture anything that will first tighten and then release your muscles.

You can also add music to this activity if you like. Try to find music without words, or music that is especially soothing to you so you aren't distracted. You might want to first try this activity without music, and then add it later.

Once you've got the whole body relaxation activity down pat, you can concentrate on any one area of your body whenever you need to. You can also do this activity anywhere and anytime you need without anyone knowing. Whether you are in school, hanging out with friends, or eating dinner with the family, you can tighten and relax your muscles to calm your body and let go of stress. No one will notice—except for the shoulders and head part; you might have to save that for when you are alone in your room.

This activity will help you realize that you have the power to release tension from each part of your body, which can help the anger to subside. This activity helped Katie control the stress and anger triggered by a perfectly normal comment she heard at school. It helped her focus her mind and relieve her body of stress.

*One day in school a friend was innocently talking about her
mom being a "pain." It just made me so angry. Why doesn't
she appreciate her mom? She doesn't know what it's like to
not have a mom. I felt myself starting to cry. Since I didn't
want to cry in school, I did this activity, and it helped me
concentrate on my body instead of my feelings. I didn't end
up crying. No one knew what I was doing; it made me feel
like I had some control over something at least, like I had
something to take away the stress of it all.*

Understanding Your Angry Body

Emma also had experiences with her angry body in her grief.
Sometimes, without meaning to be hurtful, friends and others
who are trying to be helpful can make us incredibly angry, and
our body responds. Listen to how Emma's body felt her anger.

*When I got back to school after my little sister's funeral,
someone actually said to me, "I know exactly how you feel.
My dog died yesterday."*

*Seriously? I wanted to punch her, and I never felt that way
before. But my fists clenched, my jaw locked up, and my heart
was going a mile a minute. She walked away before anything
happened.*

*I was left standing there, full of rage. Hitting her wouldn't
have made it better; it would have just gotten me in trouble
and hurt my parents more. My brother was already "the angry
one"—not me.*

Emma's experience is a common one. When one is hurt and grieving, even the most softhearted, gentle person can react with anger to an unintentionally stupid comment. Our angry feelings overwhelm us, our brain's fight reaction is triggered, our body's stress response kicks in, and we think we are going to lose control. These are all normal responses to grief. Yet hearing that anger is a normal reaction doesn't help us figure out what to do with that anger. It doesn't tell us how to express the anger or release it from our bodies in a way that won't make us angrier or get us in trouble. Our fists clench, our heart beats faster, our face feels hot, and our stomach tightens when the body's stress response is triggered.

Anger Triggers

Triggers are what set off strong emotions; our senses usually activate them, and they are unique to each individual. Triggers are like lightning bolts generated from the memory and emotion centers of our brain; they can seemingly come out of nowhere. When something triggers anger around loss, be it a song on the radio, a certain smell, seeing a photo of the person who died, or having a conversation about the person, our brain sends stress hormones throughout our body to give us the energy to "fight." Triggers are an automatic bodily response to stress.

Whatever way our anger gets triggered, we need a way to release the stress energy from our body. The following activities may help you express and release some of the angry feelings that lead to the stress response.

3.2 Anger Ball Fight!

You'll need some heavy-duty markers and several sheets of notebook paper for this activity. You will be writing down or drawing out your anger, so get as many sheets of paper as you think you might need.

1. Write down an angry feeling, angry word, or angry thought on a piece of paper. You can also draw your anger if it has shape. Your anger might be big and dark across the whole page, or maybe it's just a tiny little word in the middle. Just put down the first thing that comes to your mind or body. When we're angry, sometimes it just helps to *say it*—say what it is that you are angry about. Writing down what or who you're angry at or how angry you are gives you a chance to get the anger out of your body, off your heart and mind, and onto something else.

2. Now, as furiously and angrily as you can, crumple the paper into a tiny ball, like you're making a snowball. Then draw or write down your anger again and make another one of these "anger balls." And another. Crumple up as many of them as you think you need or want. Every time you make one and crumple it up, *notice* what you are feeling. How is your body responding? Are you getting more tense and angry? Are you feeling less or more stressed? Anxious or tired? Is your heart rate going up or down?

3. Pile your anger balls next to you on one side of the room. Now, one by one, throw them across the room toward the opposite wall. You need to be far enough away that, despite using all the strength your angry body has, you can't quite hit the far wall. The paper balls are too lightweight to sail across the room and don't have enough momentum to get to the wall.

4. Once you've thrown all the anger balls, catch your breath and notice how you feel. While doing this activity, you use your large muscles, accelerated heart rate, and rapid breathing to release the stress energy from your body. This is a particularly good activity when someone says something hurtful or stupid about your loved one or your grief. Write down what this person said, and throw it across the room. You can also just rip your anger balls apart—shred them into itty-bitty pieces and let them float like snowflakes over the wastebasket.

The anger ball activity may wear you out, exhausting your body but relieving it of its tension, especially in your legs and arms. Or you may feel so ridiculous trying to throw the anger balls across the room that you fall down laughing but relaxed. Some of the thoughts and feelings that show up on paper may surprise you; there may be anger you are holding in your body that you didn't realize. The significance of this activity is the ability it has to release muscle tension—feelings and thoughts that can only cause more pain if you continue to hold them in your body, your mind, or your heart.

While doing the anger ball activity, Matt discovered that he had been holding on to a lot of feelings about his friend. Keeping them buried and unexpressed was not helping him feel better or be less angry. The anger continued to build tension and stress. If he hadn't discovered release through the activity, he might have found himself letting the anger out in destructive and hurtful ways in the future.

I was surprised at just how many things and how many people I was mad at after JR died. I just kept getting another

*sheet of paper, smashing it up, and then another and another.
I didn't realize I had that much anger built up inside. I went
way back, to times when I could have helped JR and didn't,
times he screwed up or didn't take help that was offered.
There was a lot of buried anger in me that could have stayed
buried a long time.*

Here is another similar activity. It, too, allows you to express angry feelings, thoughts, words, or images held in your body that cause stress reactions. This one may take a little more time and thought to finish, or you may want to do it several times.

3.3 Anger Wall

You'll need a small (roughly 3 feet by 3 feet, or bigger), flat board and plain white fabric (an old pillow case or sheet will do). Tightly staple or duct-tape the fabric on the board so it creates a smooth writing surface. Use washable (not permanent) markers to write on it.

1. Write or draw whatever angry feelings, thoughts, or pictures you have inside. Notice how your body feels as you decide what you want to write or draw. If it's tight, loosen up a bit by wiggling around a little or bouncing up and down on your feet. If your heart is racing fast, slow it down with a few long, deep breaths. Then just let the marker take over.

2. As you write or draw your angry feelings, thoughts, and pictures, other feelings will probably pop up; add them to your wall. It may take a couple of days, perhaps even a month, to fill your "anger wall" with all that's been brewing inside of you. Think about how and when you heard the news about your loved one's death, what happened at the funeral, and what it's like to live without that person. Don't leave anything out; if you're angry because you're

stuck doing the dishes every night now that your mom's dead, or all anyone thinks or talks about is your dead baby sister, write it down. No one knows but you what makes you angry about the death of someone close to you. Write it all down.

3. Once you feel you've expressed much of your anger with words or drawings, check in again with your body. Do you feel less stressed? Calmer? Is your heart rate still fast? How do your muscles feel? You may have released enough of the stress now that the fight response has faded, or you may feel even more stressed having brought up all the ways and reasons you're angry. Either way, you can take this activity up a notch if you like.

4. *With an adult's permission*, get a dozen eggs or make a bunch of water balloons. Take your wall outside and lean it up against a tree away from anything that you don't want getting messy. With eggs or balloons, one by one pelt your anger wall. Really put some physical energy into it. Wind up like you are an all-star pitcher, and smack the wall. Make noises, grunt, and scream. Put a voice or a sound to your anger!

5. Aim for a particular feeling, thought, or picture and let 'er rip until all the eggs or balloons are gone. You'll probably notice now that your large muscles have released their energy and tension; your legs and arms might even feel a little wobbly. You may laugh through the whole thing, particularly if you miss the board and send an egg or balloon into the—hopefully not crabby—neighbor's yard.

6. Take a look at your wall now. All the angry feelings, thoughts, and pictures are blurred and have run; they're faded and hard to read. The feelings, thoughts, and pictures are still there—they don't go away that easily—but they are now softer, less harsh, and less intense.

You can make anger walls in many different ways. Pin your angry feelings, thoughts, and pictures to a bulletin board and release your physical energy by stabbing the pins in and out of the angry words and pictures. You can use a chalkboard and then scribble through whatever you've written, or erase it and start all over. Or you can make an anger wall journal for more private messages. Keeping a journal will also give you a chance to look back and see how your feelings or grief have changed over time.

You can make any of the activities in this book fit what feels right for you. Remember Emma's angry collage? She decided to release her angry feelings and images by burning the collage in the campfire. Her brother, however, found the anger wall helpful.

> My brother just kept getting angrier and angrier after my sister died. Mostly he'd sulk in his room, but one day he got so mad he tore the door off his bedroom like some green superhero monster. My mom and dad took us to a grief camp after my brother lost it on the door. We did the anger wall and— Whoa!—he blamed himself for what happened. That's why he was so angry. That was a big breakthrough for the Hulk.

Anger can build up in our body to the point that we actually feel Hulk-like—to the point that there's so much stress running through our bodies, blood rushing through our veins, that we don't feel as much physical pain and our muscles are tenser and stronger. Take a lesson from the Hulk and pay attention to your anger. Find healthy ways to slowly vent it from your body. Remember to *notice* how you feel in the moments before you do an activity and then again afterward. Did the activity help you express and release your body's anger?

Remember to be embodied, that is, to know what's going on in your own body. Be sure that you are getting relief and not increasing your anger when you do these activities. Noticing how your body responds will give you a good idea of what helps and whether you should try a certain activity again, in the future, when your anger is triggered.

Anger's Cousins

Closely related and oftentimes underlying our strongest anger responses are feelings of blame and shame or guilt and regret. These, too, are very normal and common responses to grief, but they are seldom talked about, and rarely are people given a way to find relief from these feelings. These "cousins" can get under our skin and in our minds and hearts, but mostly they get into our bodies.

Katie felt guilty because she was angry at her mom for leaving her to live life without her. Matt regretted having had a big argument with JR right before he died and not answering his texts the night he died. He couldn't tell anyone about either thing because he was so ashamed, and he considered suicide himself. Emma's brother blamed himself for his sister's death; his shame about what he thought he did overwhelmed him, and his reactions to that shame overwhelmed his family.

You too may have feelings of blame, shame, guilt, or regret. Maybe you blame the people you think are responsible for your loved one's death: the doctor who couldn't cure her, the drunk driver who killed him, or the drug dealer who sold her the poison. You can be so angry at these people that you want to get even—make them pay for what happened. Consider this ancient proverb attributed to the Chinese teacher Confucius: "When you start on a journey of revenge, dig two graves, one for your enemy and one for yourself." Don't let anger and revenge over your loved one's death take over your mind, body, or heart.

Blame and Shame

It's important to start with the twin feelings of blame and shame, because they will take you down a slippery slope if you don't address them. Blame and shame are emotions we take very personally. They lead to the personal belief "I am *bad*"— not "I've done something bad," but "I myself am bad." Emma's brother finally revealed what he had been sulking about for so long when—body full of rage—he tore his bedroom door off its hinges.

> When he slammed the bedroom door down, we all stood there in shock at how strong and how mad he was. Then he cried out that it was all his fault. He and dad had built the slide the summer before, and because he wanted to go be with his friends, in a hurry, he hadn't installed one of the screws tight enough. He was sure Sophie's hoodie got caught on that specific screw. He was so ashamed that he tried to hide himself under the door calling himself a murderer.

The anger cousins that are blame and shame filled Emma's brother so full of self-hate and rage that his body couldn't contain them anymore, so it ripped the door right off its hinges. Matt, too, blamed himself for JR's death and for not knowing how serious his friend's depression was.

I couldn't take it anymore. I was so angry at JR, and at the same time I was mad at myself. I should have answered his text, but I didn't; I blamed myself—for a long time.

In both cases, it's easy to see how both boys blamed themselves and felt ashamed. Such reactions are common among those who are grieving. If you feel that you are even the tiniest bit to blame or are ashamed of yourself in any way, try the following activities and see if they help.

3.4 Wearing the Mask

You'll need one piece of heavy card stock and drawing implements (pens, crayons, markers). Notice how your body feels throughout this activity, especially during steps 2 and 3.

1. Cut the paper into an oval shape. Cut out two eyes and a mouth. Draw in a nose. This is your mask. This is how the world sees you and how you present yourself to the world.

2. Decorate the mask with words, pictures, colors, or designs that depict how you think the world sees you. In the case of Emma, she might write "big sister" or "good girl" or maybe "perfect" across the forehead. Emma's brother, on the other hand, might color his mask groon with red slashes or write the words "anger" or "murderer" across it.

3. Turn the mask over and draw what your real feelings are, not what you think the world sees. Decorate the inside of the mask to reflect how you see yourself. Emma might write ugly words, use angry colors, or draw red fists. Emma's brother might draw tears of sadness or color the whole inside black.

4. Take a few deep breaths and read the following out loud:

Behind the Mask

There are 7.4 billion masks we wear.

Who the world sees

Is not who we want to "be."

Our mask is how the world treats us,

The things said and done

That began the layers and layers

Of who we've "become."

There are 7.4 billion masks we wear.

Masks of shame,

Masks of fear, anguish and blame,

Inside and out.

Wearing a mask is the game.

Our mask is how the world plays us.

The Mask Game—

Not real, not even fake.

Just the mask we make

So the world won't break us.

There are 7.4 billion masks we wear.

When will we let the world see

What's behind the mask?

Me. Just me.

See me.

Without the mask.

Consider these words carefully as you examine how it is you feel on the inside. Think about how your thoughts and feelings—how the bigger world—forms the "you" behind and in front of the mask. We all need the self-protection of the Mask Game from time to time, but the outside of the mask is not who we are meant to be, rather it is how the world sees us and how we see ourselves *in this moment in time.*

Place your mask where you can see it, along with the last verse of the poem. Over the next few days or weeks, take time to read the verse and move the mask further from your sight; eventually, you will be without the mask.

3.5 Talk to the Doc

If you believe that you caused a disease or made an illness worse by something you did (forgot to cover your mouth when you coughed or didn't wash your hands before shaking someone's hand), or if you think your anger is out of control, try this activity. You'll need your parent or guardian to make a doctor's appointment with your family doctor for a physical. If you're particularly brave, you can tell your parent or guardian that you're concerned about depression and aggression (doctor speak for "grief" and "anger").

1. Make a list of all the things you think you are to blame for in the death of your loved one. It may be very difficult to get all this on paper and could stir up strong emotions, so it is a good time to practice activity 1.3 (pause to breathe), 2.2 (your beating heart), or 3.1 (whole body muscle relaxation).

2. Put together a medical question related to each item on the list, something the doctor can answer directly. For example, if you're feeling *I'm to blame for my friend's suicide, I should have known,* ask the doc, "Is it easy to tell if someone is going to attempt suicide?

What medical conditions could my friend have had that would lead him to kill himself? How can you prevent someone from suicide? What can I do if I feel like hurting myself?"

3. Bring your list with you to your appointment and pull it out first thing. Let the doctor know right away that you have questions for him or her and you want to be sure he or she allows time for you to ask them.

4. Be sure the doc satisfactorily answers your questions; you should have a better or different understanding of the concerns on your list, and hopefully you'll feel some sense of relief from blame or a lifting of the shame you've felt. If not, if you don't feel like you understand better what happened and how or why you feel like you're to blame, try a different doctor. Or ask the doctor to refer you to a grief counselor who can help you sort through the blame and shame. Then have your parent or guardian make an appointment as soon as possible.

It is not weak or wrong to seek professional help when your body's stress response is causing you pain and discomfort. If your leg was broken, you wouldn't be concerned about seeing a doctor, would you? When your heart is broken, when you want to hurt yourself because you hurt badly or you have yourself convinced that you're a bad person, you also need professional help.

With the help of family and friends and the activities in this book, you can get through most of the responses your body has to grief. However, when the level of blame or shame you may feel regarding the death of a loved one is so intense it causes you to want to hurt yourself or die too, get help—right away.

Guilt and Regret

Guilt and regret are two feelings that come with a lot of baggage, making them very heavy and hard to handle. They are different from blame and shame because they center around behaviors—"I did a bad thing, and I could have done something better"—rather than personal thoughts we have about ourselves. Sometimes we can fix what we did, make amends, and repair relationships, but often we don't get that chance.

Guilt and regret are often called the "unfinished business" of sudden death. Things you didn't get to say or do, things you wish you would or wouldn't have said—or maybe a fight you had—can leave you feeling like you will hold on to the guilt and regret the rest of your life. Storing these kinds of feelings, and the stress they produce in your body, can only harm you now and in the years to come. If you have unfinished business you'd like to finish now instead of carrying it into the future, try this activity.

3.6 Rocks of Regret

You'll need a permanent marker and rocks that are smooth enough you can write on them. These are your "rocks of regret."

1. Write a word or make a drawing on the rocks to depict what it is you regret. Consider all the woulda, coulda, shouldas you can think of about your loved one. What is it you wished you'd said or not said, done or not done?

2. Mark up as many of the regret rocks as you want. You may have a pile of rocks, or maybe, like Matt, you have only one big, heavy rock on which you've written one big word.

3. Now take your regret rocks and put them in your pocket or your backpack. Walk around a while carrying the regret rocks and feeling their weight on your body. How long you carry them is up to you.

4. When you are ready, or when you can't hold the weight of the regrets any longer, throw the rocks into a body of water, down a hill, or into the woods. Release the regret rocks in whatever manner seems appropriate, and feel the weight lift. Notice how much lighter your body and, hopefully, your mood become.

Guilt and regret are the weights we carry. We can choose to carry the burden for a lifetime, waiting for release, but hopefully this activity shows you that you don't need to hold on to them. You can finish the business of regret and guilt. Sometimes we want to remember our regrets and feelings of guilt in order to not have them happen again. Keeping them in our memory is different than letting them weigh us down in our day-to-day lives. Matt found a great way to remember his regret but not hold on to it.

My regret rock is a boulder. One word is written across it: unanswered. I carried it in my backpack a few days. When I couldn't hold on to it anymore but didn't want to let it go either, I sat it outside my bedroom window—to remind me. Whenever I start feeling like I could have saved JR or it's my fault he died because, like so many other times, I didn't answer his text right away, I see that rock and remember how heavy it was to carry and how good it felt to throw it down. The rock reminds me that the regret is still there, but I just don't have to carry it around with me every day.

Regret and guilt can take hold of our bodies—and our lives especially—if we think there are legitimate reasons to feel responsible for a loved one's death. Rarely are we truly responsible, but we feel or believe that we somehow could have made a difference or should have done something. Feeling this way is normal, but these feelings can build up in your body if you don't find a way to release them. The rocks of regret activity shows us firsthand the heaviness of anger. The next activity is another way to release the physical energy that builds up when we hold regrets and guilt.

3.7 Chop Wood

You'll need a quiet space with enough room to swing your arms side to side and up and down without hitting anything. This activity requires some imagination on your part.

1. Stand with your feet shoulder width apart, facing straight ahead like you are on a pair of skis. Plant your feet firmly on the ground; feel the balls and heels of your feet rooted to the floor. Imagine that you have roots growing out of your feet keeping them strongly connected to the earth. It helps if you are barefoot.

2. Imagine there is a chunk of wood between your feet, and on this piece of wood is a word of guilt or regret that you feel. See the word clearly written on the piece of wood.

3. Now clasp your hands together in front of you, and as you breathe in, deeply raise your hands above your head. As you release your breath with a big, long exhale, let your hands fall down between your feet as if you are chopping that piece of wood in half. See it and the word split into pieces.

4.   Try this as many times as you need with whatever words or pictures you like. Be sure to add some sound, a grunt or a sigh, and really put some energy into chopping that wood.

Like activity 3.6 (rocks of regret), this activity is a great way to release energy and let go of anger and all of its cousins. If your body doesn't get a chance to release this stored-up energy, your muscles will always be sore, your heart rate will always be fast, and you will always feel exhausted. Releasing the fight response from your body is important. Not releasing or expressing angry body sensations, or stuffing them away, can lead to major depression (Judd et al. 2013). We'll cover that topic in the next chapter.

Wrap-Up

Hopefully you now understand that anger is not only a normal response to grief but often the first feeling we have when a loved one dies. Our body responds to the news as a threat, and our fight instinct takes over, flooding our body with stress, building tension in our large muscles, and speeding up our heart rate and breathing. Learning to calm and relax our body is an important first step in controlling our anger response.

The fight response creates intense energy in our bodies that wants release. Unfortunately, releasing that anger energy can get us into trouble. Lots of angry, grieving teens end up suspended from school or start using drugs and alcohol to cover up their anger or give themselves permission to be angry. Deliberately picking fights with others and isolating oneself are other troubling ways that anger gets released. Many of these behaviors are a result of the cousins of anger: blame and shame, guilt and regret. Knowing how they affect you and what you can do to relieve their intensity can help keep you out of trouble and from hurting more than you already are.

Trying to push anger down or pretend it's not getting to you can only lead to more problems down the road, because even though your thoughts are telling you to do one thing, your feelings and your body may be automatically doing the opposite. Your body is holding on to the anger for you and will keep it a long time if you let it. And then one day your body says *enough*, and you get sick, your leg muscles stiffen, you experience constant headaches, and you may even suffer from early onset heart disease (Felitti et al. 1998).

What's Next?

With anger comes sadness. Sadness is the feeling we most associate with someone dying. Once the reality that it really did happen sinks in, and you have some answers about how the person died, you want this loved one back, and this desire heaps a lot of sadness on top of the anger. It's like anger and sadness are partners in grief, like grief is a combination of sad and mad—we get "smad." Tolerating these two big feelings together can get overwhelming. In the next chapter we will explore how you can handle smad—the mad and the sad of grief—along with ways to be sad without it feeling like it has taken over your life, your brain, and your body.

chapter 4

your sad body

Hearing my mom crying night after night, seeing my dad break down, added so much more sadness to losing Sophie. We were all just so sad for what seemed like so long.

—Emma

Sadness is the feeling we naturally connect with grief and loss. We expect people to feel sad when someone they love dies. Some of the other feelings, such as anger, come as a surprise, and sometimes the intensity and length of our sadness surprises us too. It's not unusual to move between mad and sad feelings or to have both feelings combined. I call it "smad" when you are feeling both mad and sad at the same time, or when you get mad because you are so sad, and you don't want to be sad anymore. Sometimes you show your mad feelings more easily than your sad ones, and vice versa.

It is also easy to confuse sadness and depression. We sometimes think they are the same thing, and certainly there are feelings and body reactions that suggest we are small *d* depressed when we are grieving. There are big differences between these reactions and a big *D* depression diagnosis that is a mental illness and needs professional help.

This chapter will help you understand how sadness affects our brains and our bodies. We'll look at the difference between sadness in grief and big *D* depression, and how both affect our bodies. We'll talk about suppressing your sadness and how that can lead to suicidal thoughts or self-harm behaviors. Throughout the chapter you will find ways to manage your sadness, and maybe, surprisingly, you'll even find some joy in your sadness. When you look carefully, you may find that your days are not as full of sadness as you thought, as Emma describes:

> *Even though we felt sad every day, when I looked for the happy moments I could still see the glint in my dad's tear-filled eyes, like whenever we talked about Sophie's goofiness.*

Understanding Your Sad Body

Feeling sad affects our body in easily identifiable ways. For starters, as we struggle to accept the loss and face life without the person we love, grief causes stress hormones to build up in our brain, throwing brain chemistry off balance. The muscles in our body ache from the stress hormones as well. Most grievers also notice a slump in their posture, the way they sit, or the way they walk. This slump is the result of a lack of energy. When we are sad, often we don't eat or sleep well enough, so our energy stores become depleted. Our digestive system slows down, too, causing acid to build up in our stomach, which leads to more frequent stomach pains. We often eat more junk food with little nutritional value when we're grieving, which can worsen the problems with energy level and stomachaches.

Headaches tend to be more frequent during grieving. One reason for this is the buildup of stress hormones in the brain, but dehydration is also a cause. Most people express sadness through crying, which is natural, but not paying attention to how much water you drink when you're crying a lot can cause dehydration. Expressing feelings by crying, believe it or not, helps release the stress hormones from our body, keeping us healthier and making it less likely that the hormones will create more physical and emotional problems in the future. Expressing emotions is easier or more acceptable for some, but doing it does not require a witness or audience; it only requires a willingness to participate. Whether it is watery eyes, a single tear, full-blown sobbing, or snotty-nosed, red-eyed wailing, crying relieves grief.

Some people have the mistaken notion that if you just hold back the tears and don't let your feelings out, you have control over them. To a certain degree, this is true; you can fight back tears when you need to, such as when you're in school, in the grocery store, or with friends. However, the best way to treat your grieving body and deal with the feelings you have about a loved one is to find the space and time to have a good cry, releasing those tears.

A Good Cry is Not a Bad Thing

People talk about needing to have a good cry or how much better they feel after having one, but you may feel like there's nothing good about crying; you may be tired of crying or hearing everyone else crying. Here's a different way to look at crying.

Crying is good for you because tears release stress hormones from your body, flushing tension in order to calm and soothe it. Tears of sadness have a different chemical makeup than tears of joy (Fogel 2009). Emotional tears, not the tears we get from dust or cutting onions, have meaning and feeling behind them, and they also contain pain-relieving hormones. Oxytocin is one of these hormones; it's found in new mothers and babies as they bond to each other after birth, and your body produces it when you hug another person. You may think that crying makes you weak, but in reality, since the minute you were born, crying has been a sign that you are alive, that you need something or someone in order to stay alive. And yet repeated crying can lead to dehydration, headaches, and sore eyes, as Emma found out.

My eyes hurt so much from crying, and my nose was sore from running; crying gave me a fierce headache.

Each time you find yourself crying, whether it's a good, long cry in your bedroom, the angry cry of frustration, or tearing up as you remember something about the person who died, drink a big glass of water. If you rehydrate with at least this small amount, you will find your headache quickly becomes less severe. Letting yourself fall asleep also helps make a crying headache go away, or taking yourself outside for a short walk—after you drink that glass of water!

Placing a cool washcloth across your eyes will soothe them and reduce their redness. Or you can alternate hot and cold. Fill a washcloth with ice cubes and fill a bowl with warm water and a washcloth. Place the cool cloth on your eyes for three minutes, and then switch to the warm one. Continue this until the redness and soreness go away. If you've been crying all day and your eyes hurt, cut slices from a cucumber or cooled potato (you'll need to place these in the refrigerator in advance) and place them on your eyes for fifteen minutes. Tea bags that have been steeped in hot water also help draw out the redness and relieve the ache (make sure the bag has cooled off before you put it on your eyes). While you're waiting for these to take away the redness and soreness of a good cry, take the time to do activity 3.1 (whole body muscle relaxation) to calm everything else down.

Crying doesn't take away our sadness, but it allows us to express and release it from our body. Sadness can feel like a thick, weighted blanket. It makes us want to curl up on the couch or under our covers and just lie still. We may find ourselves without enough energy to do anything but stare out the window, wipe away our tears, and get another tissue. All these activities are normal parts of feeling and expressing sadness.

One easy way to bring some energy back into your body is to get a little sunshine. Human beings need the light rays of the sun to grow food and to stay alive, but sunshine provides a lot of other benefits, especially when you are grieving, sad, or depressed. Getting out on a sunny day can significantly change your body's health, your mood, and your energy level because the sun is a source of the necessary vitamin D.

Vitamin D for Depression

Vitamin D is essential to our body for a number of reasons. It helps with mood, bone growth, and a healthy immune system.

Studies have shown that it prevents sickness, heart disease, and bone disease. However, people living north of the equator are more likely to be low in vitamin D, which can contribute to depression (Kerr et al. 2015). If you're one of these people, it's important to make sure you get enough of it.

Feeling the warmth of the sun on our skin is comforting. Our body automatically relaxes, and our skin absorbs vitamin D from the sun's UV rays. For just fifteen minutes a day, three to four times a week, go outside and soak up the sun. That short amount of time will not contribute to skin cancer, so don't worry about slathering on sunscreen; you want your skin to be able to absorb the natural vitamin D in the sun's rays. This small but regular exposure to the sun is a great source of vitamin D, but vitamin D supplements can also help if getting out in the sun regularly is not an option. Check with your doctor about how much vitamin D you can take.

Move—Out of Sadness

Sunshine is great, but at some point your body needs more than vitamin D. It also needs fresh air and movement in order to release sadness—that slumpy, dumpy feeling. When you've had a lot of sadness in your day, balance it out with movement. Without exercise, sadness can turn into depression, which we'll discuss later in the chapter. Your body is designed to move, even when it is experiencing emotional or physical pain. Moving can be especially hard when you're grieving, when your energy stores are depleted and your emotions have left you tired and weak. When all you want to do is sleep, the only way to feel better is to move!

You can start slowly, perhaps with a five-minute-long walk or a short walk to the corner and back. Don't look at this movement as merely walking to the school bus stop every day or walking to classes. Moving your body purposely, to feel better, is the intention. It's never easy to start anything new, especially something that requires physical energy when you don't feel you have any to spare. Just ease into the activity below slowly and see if you notice a difference in how you feel, physically and emotionally. Pace yourself and keep at it, and, most importantly, find what works for you.

4.1 Move!

You can do this activity alone, or better yet, ask a friend or family member to do it with you. The other person will keep you company, encourage you to keep doing the activity, and support you as you improve.

1. Determine an amount of time or a distance that you will walk today. The distance doesn't have to be far, and a minimum of five minutes is all the time that's required. Then move! Just that amount of time or distance.

2. As you start out, notice how your body feels. What thoughts and feelings are you having? Pay attention to how your body feels as you walk. Are you having a hard time picking up your feet? Are you frustrated or irritated? Notice the weather and the sounds around you as you walk.

3. When you've finished your walk, notice again how you feel. What are your thoughts about this activity? It's okay to have negative thoughts. Does your body feel the same or different? Where in your

body do you notice something different? Just notice. It might help to write the differences down when you get back home.

4. Determine the amount of time and distance you'll walk tomorrow. It's okay if it's the same amount. Keep noticing how your body feels, what your mood is like, and what thoughts you have as you repeat the activity.

5. If you can, take a friend or your dog along. Your friend or pet can provide a social connection, another important part of healing from grief.

6. After a while, you might want to walk faster or even run, creating more feel-good hormones in your brain and body and giving yourself more health benefits. Or take your phone and headphones along and listen to one of your playlists that makes you want to move.

Once you start moving, however slow the pace or short the time, you will notice that you feel slightly better when you get back from the walk than before you started. Soon you will recognize how much better you feel when you do move your body versus when you skip it. You may even look forward to it. That was Emma's experience:

Hard as it is to admit, the therapist got this one right. I hated doing this; the first five-minute walk felt like five years. I thought my sore, tired legs and body were going to give out on me. At first I was a drama queen during this activity. What got me doing it regularly was having the time to myself. Getting outside my room, away from the family, and just going away felt like a break from things.

Big D Depression Versus Grief

As big and overwhelming as our sadness feels, and as long as it seems to last, the thing that is most important to notice and understand about sadness is that it is a feeling and not a way of being. Feelings come and go; they don't last forever. With the death of a loved one, you may be sad off and on throughout the day, perhaps more than you have felt before in your life. But you still have feelings of happiness, silliness, worry, frustration, or disappointment, too, off and on throughout the day. Now if you truly do not believe you have any other feelings but sadness, then you may be dealing more with big *D* depression than grief. It can be confusing to know the difference between grief and big *D* depression, so take a look at appendix B for a comparison.

If you are seeing more checks on the "depression" side of this list, you need to talk with someone whom you trust, preferably an adult. You don't have to talk with a parent right away. If your parents are also grieving, you might feel like you don't want to "bother" them or "make things worse than they already are," thinking you're somehow protecting them from more grief by not telling them what's going on with you. Or maybe their grief is so intense that you think they wouldn't notice or care about what's happening with you, and by not telling them you are protecting yourself from more grief and loneliness. Most parents want to know what's going on with their kids, no matter what; so if you can talk to them, do it now. Otherwise a school counselor or a nurse, a pastor or spiritual leader, an aunt or uncle, or a neighbor or family friend make good confidantes. Let one of them know that you are struggling and need to talk to a doctor. Doctors or mental health therapists can determine if you are experiencing little *d* depression with sadness, which is normal with grief, or big *D* depression, a mental and physical illness that needs professional attention.

It can be scary to see and feel some of the symptoms of big *D* depression in yourself. Try to remember that it only becomes big *D* depression when you experience the symptoms all day, every day, for at least a couple of weeks without relief. Don't expect that you will suffer from big *D* depression just because a loved one dies, but be aware that it could become an issue for you. If you are diagnosed with big *D* depression or major depressive disorder and are given medication, keep in mind that there is no magical instant cure; however, there is support, and it comes from a three-legged stool approach.

Depression—A Three-Legged Stool

Most people who are grieving the death of someone they love are not suffering from diagnosed depression, but if you have any questions about it, get a doctor or a mental health professional to screen you. If you are diagnosed with depression, keep in mind that you will recover. You will recover sooner if you follow the three-legged stool approach.

1. First leg: Diagnosed depression generally requires anti-depressant medications. Be certain to talk with your doctor very carefully about side effects and the proper dose and time to take medications. Ask when you will see results from the medication or what to do if you experience side effects.

2. Second leg: Diagnosed depression is resolved much quicker with talk therapy. Finding a therapist who has

training in grief and loss specifically and works with adolescents will be important. If you don't connect with the first therapist you see, ask him or her to refer you to someone else. Do this until you find a person who will listen and not try to fix, who will advise and not instruct, and who will understand and accept how you feel.

3. Third leg: Physical exercise is an important part of recovering from diagnosed depression (Aan het Rot, Collins, and Fitterling 2009). You'll need at least thirty minutes of exercise most days of the week. Exercising this amount of time increases the chemical serotonin, the brain's naturally produced antidepressant, and norepinephrine, the brain's chemical that stimulates positive mood. Exercising outside in the sunshine will increase your vitamin D levels and really boost your mood.

These three "legs" are going to be what support you as you resolve the diagnosed depression. One or two on their own will not be as effective and may increase the length of time it takes to reduce your symptoms. You don't have to keep feeling bad; there is help, even if seeking help feels hopeless.

A few weeks after JR's suicide, Matt's feelings of blame and anger shifted to feelings of hopelessness and helplessness. His perspective on life became *What's the use?* Soon Matt's grief and sadness intensified to the point he stayed in bed all day, every day he could. He wasn't eating and had no energy. Matt's mom waited a couple of weeks for things to get better, and when they didn't, she made him a doctor's appointment. Seeing the doctor really turned things around for Matt.

*So I ended up on antidepressants for a while. I just couldn't
get out of bed and didn't want to do anything—at all.
Therapy was not easy, but it did change things. I started to
feel alive again, started to feel some hope, a light at the end of
a tunnel.*

Matt's doctor assessed his risk for suicide, which can be a
symptom of depression and is part of its diagnosis. Matt's anger
and sadness had turned inward, and his symptoms of depression had escalated to the point that he wanted to take his own
life to relieve his pain.

*Before I got help, the depression made me so weak and tired,
I thought I may as well just join JR rather than keep feeling
this bad. There were a few times when I thought I couldn't
live with the sadness anymore.*

Suicide Risk

Matt was brave enough to talk to his doctor about his feelings
and how he was thinking about suicide. Together, they got help
for Matt. Thoughts of suicide are not a normal part of grief or
sadness, but a lot of grieving and depressed people have them.
Reach out for help if you feel like life is not worth living; if you
think others would be better off without you; if you think, as
Matt did, that the difficult, sucky feelings you're having are just
too much or are lasting too long. Let a professional determine
if you are big *D* depressed or just sad, and accept the help and
advice he or she offers. Those who love you will be grateful.

Research indicates that 90 percent of people who die by
suicide have a mental illness or a substance-abuse diagnosis

(Substance Abuse and Mental Health Services Administration 2010). Besides depression symptoms, suicide risk behaviors can be tricky to spot. Appendix C has a list of risks for suicide and includes the national hotline for preventing suicide. If you or someone you care about exhibits any of these signs, please get help—immediately. You will not give the person the "idea" of suicide if you talk about it. You may actually give that person the chance he or she was looking for to talk to someone and get help. This is a serious, life-threatening situation, and no one can get through it alone.

Here is an activity I encourage all people to do if they have had even fleeting thoughts of suicide. If you feel like the world would be better off without you, if you feel isolated and hopeless or like you can't take what the world is dishing out *right now* (remember, feelings are *not* forever), keep in mind that you have a helping hand to get you through.

4.2 My Helping Hand

Keep an open mind and heart for five minutes or less.

1. Put your hand out in front of you, palm facing out, fingers and thumbs spread.

2. Starting with your little finger, name one person in your life who loves you, who would do whatever it takes to help you. Once you've got that, fold your finger into the palm of your hand.

3. Now name someone for your ring finger. It should be someone who supports you and cares about what happens to you. Fold that finger into your palm.

4. Keep going with your next two fingers. Name a teacher at school, a coach, your neighbor—whoever comes to mind. You don't have to be superclose to this person, just name someone who you think is or would be a helper to you or anyone who needed it.

5. Your thumb represents you. You are a person with the strength and the sense to help yourself; to take care of yourself; and to notice when you need love, help, and support. Tuck "you," your thumb, under the other four fingers of love, help, and support. This fist you've made is your strength and support.

6. Take your hand and place it on your heart. Take a deep breath and think about and hold on to the "helping hand" you just created for yourself. Know that these people will always be there to help you; they're right there at the end of your arm, carried with you and in your heart all the time.

7. When you are feeling suicidal, sad, or depressed, look to your helping hand and know that these are the people who will help.

Knowing there is always someone you can count on, someone who will help you when you need support, is crucial to surviving suicidal thoughts, deep depression, and sometimes everyday life. Having a physical representation with you at all times lets you see firsthand, so to speak, that there is help out there; all you need to do is reach out and express to your helpers what you need or how you feel. For many grieving teens, that may be easier said than done when they are suppressing emotions, holding feelings in, not letting others help, or questioning whether their helpers will or can help; and it's these behaviors that lead to unhelpful, unhealthy, and even deadly actions.

Emotional Suppression and Self-Harm

Some grieving teens decide to avoid the sadness, deny the hurt feelings, ignore the memories, and stuff all of it deep down in the darkness of their brain or their heart because it is just too hard to feel the feelings, to cry, to yearn for the person, and to be reminded of that person's absence. The pain of grief and loss can feel worse than any other pain, and when teens find a way to control it, it seems like a way out of the grief. It's not. Katie didn't realize how much she was harming herself by pushing the hurt of her grief away.

> *Finding a way to relieve my pain, to control my feelings, to control anything, was the reason I stopped eating. No one could make me eat; no one could make me grieve. I had to have some control over these uncontrollable feelings. I stopped eating because I was too sad to be hungry—for anything.*

Suppressing sadness can have several negative effects on your body. As we've learned, stress can build up in your body, and if you don't find release, it can cause headaches, stomachaches, sore muscles, and even heart disease. Suppressing feelings can also turn into an eating disorder (Fogel 2009).

When Katie said she was too sad to be hungry, it meant that she had lost touch with what her body was telling her. Holding her deep feelings of sadness inside suppressed her body's natural hunger. Forcing your body to not feel and express emotions will not help you. Suppressing your body's natural processes only hurts it. If you find yourself in this situation, you need to reach out for professional help—a doctor or a grief counselor—right away.

So often, especially if you are the oldest sibling in your family, or the oldest male, you can feel as though you have to be the family's rock, or the glue that holds the family together, so you hide your sadness. Besides not eating, other self-harming behaviors, such as cutting, burning, punching, head banging, drinking, eating harmful substances, or rubbing and scratching to the point of injury, are ways that teens sometimes release the energy of intense feelings. By feeling physical pain or some sort of control over both their emotions and physical body, they may feel like they can cope with the suppressed emotional pain. These self-harming behaviors may not be suicidal, but they can be extremely dangerous. As with suicidal thoughts, you need to get help and support if you are harming yourself, especially if the following ideas for distracting yourself from these behaviors do not help.

4.3 Distract the Hurting

Mark this page or rewrite these distraction options on a sheet of paper to keep near you for when you feel the need to self-harm. Try each one to see what works. Different distractions may work on different days, but keep trying. If none of these ideas keep you from hurting yourself, get professional help as soon as possible.

- Take a cold shower or bath. The cold stimulates your nervous system.

- Squeeze ice for the same reason; it is distracting to hold on to slippery ice.

- Hold a bag of frozen food.

- Write down your feelings. If they're angry feelings, try doing activity 3.2 (anger ball fight).

- Get your mind full. Pay attention to your body and your breath as you take ten deep breaths, or try some of the activities of activity 2.3 (making sense).

- Eat one thing mindfully. Eat a single raisin for at least one minute. Pay attention to everything about eating the raisin—what it tastes like, your teeth grinding on the surface, the smell and texture. Stay focused on eating the raisin (see "Savor the Sweetness" in activity 2.3, making sense.)

- Take a long, warm shower or bubble bath.

- Gently spread lotion on whatever area of your body you intended to hurt or have hurt in the past.

- List one hundred things that make you happy.

- List the top ten good things about yourself.

- Put together a five-hundred-piece jigsaw puzzle.

- With an adult's permission, bang pots and pans together as loudly and for as long as you can.

- Rip up old newspapers, magazines, or phone books.

- Bite into a hot pepper or chew on a piece of gingerroot.

- Stomp your feet on the ground for as long as you need to.

- Draw a sketch of yourself or find a photo and mark where on your body you hurt or want to hurt yourself.

Getting the Sad Out

There are several activities in this chapter and book that will help you express your feelings and get the hurt out without hurting more or differently. Suppressing your feelings, trying to keep them in, or diverting them with a different kind of pain will not ease the hurt. Grief is something you have to go through in order to get through it; holding on to your grief and pain adds more grief and pain.

You can express your sadness and release its intensity through art. Creating a memory scrapbook, photo album, or collage using photos of your loved one is a great way to release sadness. You may cry while working on these projects, but you will also remember sweet moments with the person who died. Over time, you will find that your sadness subsides a bit as you look at these memory projects, and your memories will bring smiles. So often there are no words to capture our sadness or our memories or all that happens when a loved one dies; however, these projects can speak the words that we can't speak right now.

4.4 There Are No Words

You may want to gather magazine photos, images from the Internet, your own photos, crayons, markers, glue, scraps of colored paper, scraps of material or old clothes your loved one wore, coloring books, or sketchbooks to have on hand for these projects.

Memory book. Begin by placing photos of your loved one in the pages of a journal, sketchbook, or scrapbook. You can include other images you have collected, words, or quotes that have meaning for you. Flowers from the funeral, a scrap of your loved one's favorite clothing, or a poem may also express your emotions.

Photo collage. On a piece of poster board or in a large-format blank journal, glue either magazine photos, images from the Internet, or your own images to create a collage that expresses your sadness. The images should express what you sense, feel, or think, or how your body feels. If you find words in magazines that seem to fit the images, glue them throughout your collage, or you can write them with a marker or crayon.

Coloring. You may not be ready to start a project as involved as a memory book or collage just yet, so start small. Grab some crayons and paper or a coloring book—there are now many adult coloring books to choose from. Spend ten minutes or so coloring. The movement of your hand, seeing the colors, and smelling the familiar smell of crayons will lower your heart rate, slow your breathing, and calm you down. Coloring works very well after you've been crying.

Memory makers. If you know someone who sews, ask if he or she can make something using an article of clothing that reminds you of your loved one. You might like a heart-shaped pillow, a stuffed teddy bear, or even a quilt. If you don't know anyone who sews, search the Internet for craftspeople who do these kinds of projects and contact them. When you get your memory maker back, add a soothing or familiar scent or color to the item, such as a drop of your loved one's perfume or a smattering of his or her favorite color. A few drops of lavender oil will calm and soothe you. You may find yourself stroking your memory maker, holding it close to your face or over your heart. All these sensations are ways of helping your body heal.

You may be surprised at how using your sense of sight, creativity, imagination, and curiosity in these ways shifts your mind and body toward a new way of being. All these memory-making activities are bittersweet, because they remind us of sweet, happier times with the person we love and the bitter sadness we feel knowing that this person is now gone from our everyday life. These activities can teach us that joy and sadness are both part of life.

Finding Joy and Happiness

Sadness is not the opposite of joy or happiness. These emotions are all part of life. However, living in a home filled with sadness can be too much at times. It's okay to escape the sadness and have fun or be happy even when you feel grief. Doing so does not disrespect the person who died, take away your grief, change what happened, or mean you are heartless or horrible. You are human, and humans can only take so much sadness before they need to find relief, even when someone they love has died.

When it seems as though every day is a sad day, find a way to also see joy and happiness. Doing so will take your concentrated effort. Give the search just a few minutes each day, if that's all you can spare or think you can bear.

Fake It 'til You Make It

There has been a ton of research on the subject of smiling and the impact it has on our lives. You may have heard the saying that it takes more muscles to frown than it does to smile, and it's true. You may have also heard the saying "Fake it 'til you make it." What do these things mean, and how might they affect our sadness?

Just *pretending* to be happy can make you happy. Smiling even when you don't feel it, when you are faking it, can change your sad feelings. Smile studies by Robert Zajonc (1989) found that if you place a pencil in your mouth to trick your facial muscles into smiling, your brain sends more blood to those muscles, which signals our brain to a change in mood. Try it. With or without the pencil, let yourself smile. Here are some other ideas of ways to induce smiling and experience some joy when you feel sad.

4.5 Joy's Turn

Let go of sadness for just a few minutes once a day in one of these ways.

- Watch à video showing crazy cat behavior or babies laughing.

- Put on your favorite tune and dance with no one watching.

- Sneak away to a playground and watch how little kids enjoy life.

- See a sweet movie that you know has a happy ending.

- Search YouTube for "laughter yoga" videos and play along.

- Buy yourself or someone else flowers.

- Eat just one cookie, slowly, while smiling.

- Find images on the Internet of three places you'd love to travel to someday, and then dream about being in these places.

- List ten things that bring you joy.

It really is okay to smile again, even to laugh through your tears. It's okay to set aside sadness, because it will be there again. Sadness is part of what your mind, your heart, and your body need while you're grieving, but setting aside your sadness while taking care of your body and finding joy are also part of healing grief. It's important to allow yourself to express all of your feelings and give your body what it needs.

Wrap-Up

This has been a full and intense chapter. We looked at sadness and the effect it has on our body and behavior. The more we know about sadness, little *d* and big *D* depression, suicide, self-harm, and suppression of intense feelings, the better we can help ourselves and others we care about. Sadness is something that everyone experiences in life. It can be scary to have such intense feelings, and perhaps this is the first time you have felt this deeply sad. The one thing to always keep in mind is that the sadness will pass; its intensity will lessen. Even though profound sadness will enter your life, you can and will find joy and happiness again.

What's Next?

Losing someone we love, wanting this person back again, and wondering if we'll lose more people can bring on a loneliness that feels like it will never go away. In the next chapter we'll look at feelings of loneliness and being alone, exploring how to find a community and friends and make connections with others who are grieving and feeling the same loneliness.

chapter 5

your lonely body

Our house was so quiet. Everyone stayed in their rooms. If we did eat together, no one talked. I counted seven meals in a row where none of us said anything. You could almost taste the loneliness. I couldn't talk to my friends about it; they didn't get it, and I couldn't stand the look of pity on their faces. Couldn't talk about it at home either. How do you talk about your feelings to zombie parents or rage-machine brothers?

—Emma

We didn't have a funeral for her; she was cremated. My dad brought the urn in and put it on the coffee table and went to his room. Some family came by for the next few days, but not much after that; it felt pretty lonely in our house.

—Katie

From before we're even born, we are connected to those we love. It is the normal human condition to be attached to others; after all, we were all born attached to our mothers by an umbilical cord. We are born to be in relationships, to be social, not isolated and alone. When someone we love and are attached to dies, we feel lonely, as though there is a part of our heart and body that is missing.

There is a difference between being alone and being lonely. Sometimes we want and choose to be alone. Being alone can be comforting and can give us the time and space to think and feel and figure things out. Being lonely, however, isn't a choice; it's a feeling of loss and abandonment, a desire to be with someone when we can't. Even when you're in a crowd of people, loneliness can leave you feeling isolated. Emma defines loneliness as sitting night after night at her family's dinner table with no one noticing each other or connecting in any way. Emma describes it as feeling abandoned by family members. Loneliness usually involves feelings of isolation, as if you are all alone in your grief even when your friends and family are around you. However, feelings of loneliness are unique to each person.

According to statistics gathered for Children's Grief Awareness Day, one in five children experience the death of a loved one before the age of eighteen. A survey of one thousand teens found that 90 percent of them had lost a loved one. One out of every twenty teens will lose a parent or parental figure before graduating from high school. Roughly seventy thousand children die every year, and 83 percent have siblings who survive. That means there are many more grieving teens out there besides you; you are not alone, though you may feel incredibly lonely.

When the National Alliance for Grieving Children polled grieving teens in 2011 and 2012, 33 percent of them said their current guardian found it hard to talk to them about any personal stuff. This could explain what was happening with

Emma's family. Fifty-nine percent found it helpful to spend time with friends, though 52 percent found it difficult to talk to their friends about their grief. These statistics show how easy loneliness and isolation can become a part of your grief process and your life, especially if your friends aren't grieving or have never had to deal with the loss of a loved one.

Isolating yourself in your room, hiding your feelings from others, or pretending things are okay when they're not only adds to your loneliness and prolongs your grief. Matt thought he was the only one missing his friend JR.

> I tried to think of a single day, since third grade, when I didn't talk to JR or didn't hang out with him. I couldn't think of one single day, and now, every day, it's just me—alone. No one knows how it feels to lose something you had every single day.

This chapter will look at how feelings of loneliness affect your body and how making connections with other grieving people helps heal loneliness. Reconnecting with your body, your family, and your friends is an important part of moving through grief. It's important to know and remember that 41 percent of those teens polled by the NAGC said that talking to others who have gone through grief was helpful, and the same percentage said that attending a grief group helped. We'll explore what kinds of community grief support you may have available that can help relieve the isolation and loneliness you're feeling. We'll also look at social media, which can help you find a community of people who understand loneliness—not just "friends," but connections with others who are feeling what you feel.

Understanding How Loneliness Affects Your Body

Loneliness, isolation, and rejection have a powerful effect on us from the beginning of our life. Going back to infancy, each of us was connected to another human being, our mother, for nine months before we were born. And for most of us, we remained connected to our mother throughout our early years. When babies are orphaned and grow up without the loving contact of a mother, they can wither away physically from the loneliness and lack of attachment to another human being and eventually die (Bowlby 1969). Teens and adults similarly suffer when the death of a loved one severs a connection. Older people who are lonely after the death of a spouse, a child, or a friend have a much higher risk of developing Alzheimer's disease, heart disease, and depression, which can lead to premature death (Bennett et al. 2006). Researchers have proven that the surge of stress hormones caused by losing a loved one, or being broken-hearted, can cause chest pains and heart attack–like symptoms in even the healthiest of individuals. It's called broken heart syndrome.

These same stress hormones are released in our body when we feel lonely, isolated, or rejected, and they cause a number of painful and chronic physical symptoms. Studies have shown that isolation and loneliness can increase the risk of death as much as smoking or obesity (Holt-Lunstad, Smith, and Layton 2010). When looking at images of the brains of people who felt rejected, researchers found that most of the brain activity occurred in the same part of the brain that processes a burn injury, one of the most painful physical traumas a human being can experience (Kross et al. 2011). As you can see, loneliness, isolation, and rejection have a significant impact on our physical well-being.

Loneliness, isolation, and rejection can affect our physical body from the time we are born into old age, and feeling these things when you're already grieving can be incredibly painful. Across our life span, to stay generally healthy we need a good diet, exercise, mental stimulation, and—most importantly—social connection. To help you find a way out of loneliness, let's look at ways to find communities of grieving people.

Finding Grieving Communities

No one wants to go to a grief group or a grief camp. They are the "clubs" no one wants to belong to. Do you have visions of people sitting in a circle talking about their feelings while passing around tissues? A grief group or grief camp may sound like less fun than just about anything you can imagine. In reality, however, these groups and camps likely differ markedly from your assumptions. Anyone who runs a grief group or grief camp knows that you can't help kids and teens, much less keep them coming back, if all you do is sit around and talk about grief. Emma discovered that her assumptions had been wrong all along, and her experience is quite common.

> When we first started going to the grief group, I was scared and felt stupid and afraid that I wouldn't find anyone there who could understand. Boy, was I wrong. I found friends that I know I will have the rest of my life.

Grief groups and camps are designed to fit the needs of those who attend and to keep them interested. These groups and camps have a ton of interesting and fun things to do to counteract loneliness and rejection, and they are the places where you will find others your age who are grieving too. Many of these people will quickly become your friends because they share some of the same feelings, reactions, thoughts, experiences, memories, and heartaches that you do.

> *Attending grief camp with my whole family surprised me. Once I got past the first few uncomfortable introductions, it was real clear that these people knew what I knew and felt what I was feeling. I felt normal and accepted immediately; that's what made our friendships so strong, even now after the camp is over.*

Emma's experience is similar to that of thousands of kids, teens, and adults who have attended a grief group or camp. Most people don't want to be there, but once they realize they are with people who understand and can share sadness and laughter and grieve together, lifelong bonds are formed. Attending a grief group or grief camp gives you an understanding that other people your age are dealing with the same feelings and experiences. Knowing you are not alone reduces the weight of your feelings and grief. The social connections and friendships you make can almost instantly relieve your loneliness. Even if you return to your school, home, or community and feel lonely there, you've now found a community that understands your grief and can help you find a way out of your loneliness.

The NAGC keeps a list of grief groups and camps around the country (https://childrengrieve.org/find-support), and you may find this link to a video of kids talking about going to grief camp helpful: www.youtube.com/watch?v=xfxXar--qhY.

Grieving with Man's or Woman's Best Friend

Pets, those furry, feathery critters we love, are another important group of beings that can help relieve loneliness. Domesticated pets have an instinctual desire to connect with humans, and they can help us through our most difficult times. They listen and let us talk when we feel like no one else will.

Animal-assisted therapy involves using trained animals (horses, cats, dogs, and even dolphins) to help people of all ages. Based on the premise that humans have been attached to animals for their survival since the beginning of time, animal-assisted therapy is used in nursing homes, hospitals, and assisted-living facilities, which all recognize that pets have the ability to lift spirits and generally make people feel better (Kahn 1997). Our own pets offer us unconditional love. Matt found that his spirits were lifted whenever his dog, Buddy, was around.

> *I gotta say my lifesaver during those dark days was my little mutt, Buddy. No matter how bad I was feeling, he seemed to know what I needed and would just be there with me.*

Pets can mirror our feelings, sense our need for closeness, and generally bring a smile to our faces. Stroking a dog's fur calms our parasympathetic nervous system; after a while we begin to breathe in the same slow rhythm as our pet (see "Pet the Dog" in activity 2.3, making sense). If you don't have a pet, look to social media and "borrow" one. Look up videos of dogs and cats on YouTube or check out websites of breeders and dream of your future pet.

Social Media Connections and Disconnections

Going online is another way to reduce loneliness and find other teens who are going through the same things as you. Social media—the number of ways we communicate with people electronically, from e-mail to Facebook—has received a lot of criticism for its ability to disconnect people from each other, because they plug into their devices instead of relating directly with people; there's a lot of research out there to prove this is the case. However, like anything, social media has both positive and negative aspects.

On the one hand, depending on the type you use and how you use it, social media can be a great way to connect with others, form a community, and lessen your loneliness. Social media can help you find other people's stories of hope and healing after grief, as well as friends, family, and others who knew your loved one. These stories and connections can reduce your loneliness. You can create your own web page or website to memorialize your loved one or to address the cause of his or her death, which may help others.

On the other hand, being alone in your room and first hearing the news of a loved one's death on social media can be devastating and shocking. Letting social media become the only form of interaction with others, or finding yourself repeatedly reading and reposting messages that intensify your sadness or loneliness, does you no good. Because social media can ease your loneliness or deepen it, it's important to remember to balance your time spent interacting with social media. It's good to disconnect from the screen once in a while.

If social media is having a negative effect on you, you'll know it. You'll find yourself staying awake late into the night with the blue haze of a screen keeping you up as you endlessly search for answers to what happened or how to get "over" this grief or for games to play to distract yourself from your feelings. You'll know you're lost in the world of social media when you can't set your tablet or smartphone aside without feeling something is wrong. When you feel like your only friends are on an electronic device, and you are isolating yourself from live human friends, it's time to unplug.

5.1 Unplug

Keep in mind that this activity is a *temporary* setting aside of social media to help you pay attention to your body and to start reconnecting socially, emotionally, and physically with others. You may want to review and repeat activity 1.3 (pause to breathe), 3.1 (whole body muscle relaxation), or 4.1 (move).

1. Leave your phone on a table in your room and go somewhere else for one hour. Because your phone may be your way of telling time, wear a watch or know where to find a clock to track the time. It's easier to get through the hour if you are physically active and if you regularly tell yourself *It's only an hour.*

2. Once you've unplugged for an hour, try unplugging for a school day. "Accidently" leave your phone at home. Throughout the day you'll want to do whatever activities calm and relax you. Also, pay attention and notice how you feel, what your bodily sensations are, and what you are paying attention to without the phone. How distracted are you? Without your phone around, what's keeping your attention?

3. When you get back to your phone, what did you miss? Did a lot happen while you were unplugged? How "big" were the things you missed? Was the time away from your phone important or unimportant?

4. Try going a whole day without your phone once a week. Remaining disconnected from your device will help you reconnect with your body and how it feels.

Reconnect with Your Body

The effects of loneliness, isolation, and rejection in our body can make us want to disappear—pretend that we don't exist. These feelings can get so big that we lose track of or disconnect from the body we inhabit. Katie felt like she was trapped in a steel box. She was isolated from her family even though they inhabited the same home; they were all afraid of their own fragility.

Once my mom died and we all went into our separate rooms, it felt like there were big, steel boxes around each of us. No one got close, no one touched each other—it was like if we hugged or held on to each other, we might all shatter into a million pieces or something.

In order to end loneliness and begin to socially reconnect with others, you need to feel strong and present in your own physical body. Katie may not have been able to get a hug from her sister or her dad, but there were ways for her to step out of the steel box and feel physically hugged.

5.2 Give Yourself a Hug

Research has proven that hugging raises the level of oxytocin, the "love hormone," in your body. Oxytocin reduces stress in the body and increases the amount of the pleasure chemical dopamine, improving your mood and tolerance for pain.

1. Take a deep breath in, and let it out.

2. Bring your right hand across your body and place it under your left arm, about three inches down from your armpit. There is a nerve point here that is part of the larger energy system of your body. Applying pressure to this point releases energy throughout your body.

3. Now take your left arm and reach it across your body, wrapping it around the top of your upper right arm.

4. Give yourself a squeeze—a hug.

5. Notice how your body feels as you gently hold yourself.

6. Breathe into the hug and hold it for a few minutes as you feel your body start to become calm. You may imagine the oxytocin running throughout your body giving you love and comfort.

You can hug yourself anywhere, anytime, without anyone knowing; it just looks like you're crossing your arms. Treat yourself to a hug whenever lonely feelings wash over you or you start to feel as if you've lost touch with your physical body. Hug yourself when you've vanished into your loneliness and isolation. Another way to feel "in" your body is to tap yourself *in*.

Tapping one side of your body and then the other, or marching in place, stimulates the cortex (thinking brain) and the limbic (emotional) brain, reconnecting them so the whole brain is activated. Grieving and feeling lonely generates a lot of activity in the limbic brain, which can stir up a lot of negative thoughts in the cortex. Tapping or stimulating both sides of your body can bring balance back to your brain and your life.

5.3 Tap In

1. Sit comfortably with both feet on the floor, hands in your lap. Be sure the room is quiet, your phone is off, and you won't be disturbed for a few minutes.

2. Take a few deep breaths.

3. Bring to your mind a positive thought about your life. Imagine your loneliness subsiding. Picture yourself connected to friends and family.

4. Be sure you have a clear picture in your mind of the positive experience; identify all the senses involved with this experience. If you are at a party with friends having a good time, hear the music being played, smell the campfire burning, taste the roasted marshmallows, and feel yourself dancing.

5. Once you have as many details as possible, begin to "tap in" to what that experience felt like. Take your hand (it doesn't matter which one) and tap your right knee and then your left, back and forth at least twenty times, or you can tap your feet, marching in place, lifting first your left leg and then your right at least twenty times.

6. You can also tap your arms or the tops of your hands, whatever feels best, keeping a steady back-and-forth, left-and-right rhythm of twenty taps.

7. Stop and take a deep breath and see how your body feels. If you feel good, tap some more. You can continue tapping as long as the positive feelings are there.

8. You can tap with any positive thought or feeling. Imagine making a new friend while tapping. Think about the pet or pets you are going to have when you are an adult, and tap in to what that will be like. Tap in to what it feels like to be part of a community of caring people who understand what it's like to lose a loved one.

9. Practice activity 5.2 (give yourself a hug) above, and tap in to that. Notice how your body feels once you have held it and tapped in to positive feelings.

Though it may seem a little silly to tap and hug yourself, scientific research has proven that both back-and-forth tapping (called *bilateral stimulation*) and applying pressure to nerve points (called *acupressure*) are effective treatments for relaxing the body and reconnecting the parts of the brain in times of stress.

Setting aside the screen, reconnecting with your body, and having positive thoughts and feelings are some of the ways to reduce isolation and loneliness, but healing from loneliness requires human contact. Here are a few ways to connect directly with others.

5.4 Making More Connections

The following suggestions will require courage, bravery, and a "just do it" attitude.

- Give someone a hug.

- Make eye contact with someone.

- Create music, join a band or a choir, or make a playlist and share it.

- Compliment someone.

- Be kind to someone (for example, open the door for the person behind you).

- Say hello to someone with a smile.

- Be generous; volunteer at a food bank.

- Write a thank-you note to someone.

- Listen to another person without thinking about what you are going to say next.

- Ask—just ask—for what you need. You may not get it, but you surely won't if you don't ask.

- Add to this list at least two more things that you can do to connect with other people.

Wrap-Up

Loneliness is a serious state of mind that affects your body, your thoughts, your feelings, your spirit, and your long-term health. Being lonely and feeling isolated or rejected can lead to serious health complications; these feelings can literally break your heart. By connecting with other grieving individuals, with communities of grieving people, with pets, with forms of social media, and with your own body, you can lessen the effect that loneliness has on your grief and your life. You can end your loneliness by simply reaching out. I say "simply," but reaching out isn't easy.

What's Next?

Fear and anxiety affect our body and can shake up everything we know, creating a future full of worry. In the next chapter we'll look at our scared body and explore ways to cope with the fear and anxiety brought on by grief.

chapter 6

your scared body

*When someone younger than you dies, it makes you wonder,
When will I die?*

—Emma

*If I was thinking of killing myself after JR died, were my other
friends thinking that too?*

—Matt

I just kept thinking, What if my dad dies too?

—Katie

When your world is turned upside down by grief, life can get
pretty scary. Matt, Katie, and Emma experienced fears that come
up for a lot of teens when life suddenly changes because of a
death. Emma started having nightmares about being buried, so
she became afraid of the dark and wondered when she would
die. Matt feared that more of his friends were going to commit

suicide, while Katie was afraid that she might end up an orphan with nowhere to go.

When you are grieving, it's natural to think about death and dying: Who else will die? What happens when you die? What if I die? Having so many unanswered questions—so many thoughts—about death can bring confusion and fear. Fear, like anger, can affect your grieving body in a number of ways.

When someone dies, the news can immediately ignite the fight, flight, freeze, faint response in your brain, sending signals throughout your body to put it on alert. Most of the time, fear generates the flight or freeze response: either your body wants to run and get away as fast as it can, or it stops in its tracks and can't seem to move.

The flight response is very similar to the fight response. Stress hormones build up in our body, saturating the large muscles in our legs and arms with adrenaline and making them almost itchy to move—to run. Our heart beats faster and our breathing increases and grows shallower. If fear makes your body want to run, look back at the activities in chapter 4, "Your Sad Body." Activities such as 4.1 (move) may help you release some of the body's built-up energy and adrenaline in order to calm your fear.

The freeze response is that "deer in the headlights" look, is going quiet, and is disappearing. Its purpose is to make us invisible to whatever is threatening us so it will go away. Because we are under threat, our body responds the same as it does for fight or flight; so even though the energy and adrenaline in our body is revving us up to protect ourselves, the freeze response bottles up all of that energy, making us scared stiff. We can be frozen with fear even if we're not quite sure what we are afraid of, or if the fear is actually in our minds and not in front of us;

for example, we may think we hear a lion in the jungle even if we can't see it.

Fear is like that monster that you used to believe was under your bed or in your closet. It can take over your mind and body until someone comes along, believes your fear is real even though the monster isn't, and "checks" under the bed or in the closet. Acknowledging the fear tames the monster of our thoughts and beliefs. In the following activity, you will have the chance to name your fear and create a mantra to help you tame it. A *mantra* is your own private motto—what you want to believe—that you repeat over and over. As you concentrate on the meaning of your mantra, it becomes your belief.

6.1 Name It to Tame It

Gather together whatever writing or drawing materials you enjoy working with. You can use an art sketchbook if you have one, your journal, or your school notebook and a pen.

1. Take a deep breath or two. Begin listing or drawing the fears you have right now, in this moment.

2. Draw or write where in your body you feel this fear and what you are thinking when you are afraid.

3. Now draw or write the opposite of what you wrote in step 1. If you are afraid of suffocating, write about or draw yourself breathing. Do the same for step 2. (See the table below for examples.) If you feel yourself breathing fast, write about or draw yourself breathing slowly and regularly.

4. Finally, write down a five- or six-word sentence that describes what you drew or wrote in step 3. Put together a sentence that describes

the opposite of your fears and worrisome thoughts. This is your mantra, which will "tame" your fears.

To help you understand this activity, here is an example of what Emma wrote.

Step 1

Emma's fears

Being buried

Suffocating

Darkness

Step 2

In my body I feel…

my chest is heavy.

my breathing is fast.

my heart beating fast.

I am thinking…

I'm going to die.

I can't catch my breath.

What's happening?

Step 3

The opposites of Emma's fears

I am alive.

I can breathe.

There is light.

In my body I feel…

all of my body.

slow, regular breathing.

warmth.

I am now thinking….

I survived.

everything is normal.

I can see now.

Step 4

Emma's mantra: **I am alive—everything is normal.**

Whenever Emma's fears creep in and she feels the sensations and believes in her mind that she is going to be buried alive, she repeats these six words to reassure herself, to tame the fear monster. Though she knows that she isn't going to be buried alive, the mantra helps her cope with the real fear she feels.

> I was shocked by how afraid I was; it was stupid, really; I knew I would never be buried alive. I knew that you can't feel anything when you are dead and buried, but I was still afraid. I didn't expect to feel that afraid of something that wasn't real.

Coping with the Unexpected

Death always feels unexpected, and the unexpected is what scares us. It shakes up our reality and sense of safety. How we thought our lives were going to be, who we knew in the world, changed suddenly and unexpectedly. Nothing after the death of a loved one seems real, and that is scary. Finding a way to get back to what is real not only tames our fear but helps heal our grief.

One way to get back to what is real is to put yourself in the present moment, not in the past and definitely not in the future, which you may have convinced yourself is scary by thinking about things such as your own death. Whenever you find yourself drifting off into the past or a frightening future, you feel like you are so scared that you're losing touch with reality, or you are getting lost in the what-ifs and the monster that is your grief and fear, try the following activity. It can help you ground yourself to what is happening now and calm your fear and anxiety. Don't let its name fool you; you're not being punished!

6.2 Get Grounded

For this activity, sit with your back as straight as you can. Imagine there is a string pulled tight to the ceiling that passes through the top of your head, down through the back of your neck, and through your spine. This is the posture you want to hold; it will help you breathe much easier. Loosen your jaw, keep your eyes open, let your hands be open in your lap, and make sure your feet touch the ground.

1. Take three deep breaths and then continue with normal breathing.

2. Without moving your body, look around and find three things in the room that are your favorite color.

3. Now listen for three sounds you hear around you; one of them can be your own breathing.

4. See if you can smell three things in the room. These might be a little tougher to identify, and that's okay. See if you can name just one.

5. Focus your attention on your feet touching the ground, your hands touching your lap, and your body sitting on the chair.

6. Take three more deep breaths.

Grief Anxiety

Anxiety is worry, and it's a normal part of life; being worried about your grades in school, about getting into college, or about your girlfriend or boyfriend breaking up with you are all normal anxious thoughts. However, *grief anxiety* develops when you think your worst fear or worry has come true, such as someone you love dying, and as a result you worry about what else may happen or how much worse a situation can get. After JR's death, Matt thought that his other friends might commit suicide, and this anxiety made him worry nonstop about them, turning into grief anxiety. Because of his anxiety about losing someone else, scary thoughts kept popping up in his head.

All I could think about was someone else dying or thinking about killing themselves. It was freaking me out. I was looking at all my friends wondering who was next. I just couldn't stop worrying about it.

Grief anxiety can get the best of our days and nights. If you are experiencing days and nights filled with worry, restlessness, and an inability to concentrate on anything else; if you feel panicked, as though your life is in jeopardy; or if you experience chest pain, heart palpitations, sweating, or chills, tell an adult right away. You may be having an anxiety attack, a much more serious experience that may require you to get help in order to calm yourself.

Whether you experience ongoing anxiety or it occurs only once in a while, keep in mind that it is all in your mind. Your thoughts create anxiety, and thoughts are temporary; you can stop your thoughts and change them. Anxious thoughts come and go; like the bubbles children blow, they always pop in the end and disappear. On some days, especially when we are grieving, it seems as though there are a million anxious, worrisome, and fearful thoughts bubbling up. Here is an activity you can try on those days, when you want the anxious thoughts to stop.

6.3 STOP IT

1. **S:** Stop all your anxious or scary thoughts now.

2. **T:** Take three deep breaths.

3. **O:** Oppose the thought and turn it around to its opposite.

4. **P:** Prepare a mantra.

5. **I:** Imagine it is true.

6. **T:** Take three deep breaths.

STOP IT is another example of an activity that looks simple but is not that easy. You will find yourself having to repeat it over and over with a single, anxious thought until the thought changes. Even when you think you have it down, these things (also known as "thinks") can pop back up when you least expect them.

A STUG, or *sudden, temporary, upsurge* of *grief*, can also pop up without warning, suddenly creating a big burst of grief or worry. Though a STUG is temporary, it doesn't feel like it is at the time, seemingly hanging on. Whenever you are getting a STUG, one way to calm the upsurge is to use the ancient form of relaxation, mindfulness, and embodiment known as yoga.

Yoga is thousands of years old; it's not a religion, rather a practice of paying attention to your mind and your body. Because yoga can calm and strengthen bodies and minds, focus attention, and relieve anxiety, it has become popular with many athletes, musical artists, and entire sports teams, as well as millions of regular folks. Here are a couple of easy yoga poses that research has found relieve anxiety, worry, and fear and calm the body and mind.

6.4 Forward Fold

Yoga can be done anywhere; just be sure you have plenty of room around you to move. Check this by standing in one spot and swinging your arms from side to side; if you don't hit anything, then you're good to go. It's usually easier to do yoga with bare feet for solid footing and comfortable clothes that accommodate stretching your body.

1. Begin standing with your feet lined up right under your hips; imagine you are on a pair of skis. Plant your feet solidly on the floor, imagining there is a triangle under each one, running from the bottom of your big toe over to your baby toe and down to your heel, then back up to your big toe. Focus on keeping all three points firmly planted. Let your arms rest at your sides comfortably. Keep your head up and imagine the string from activity 6.2 (get grounded) is keeping your posture upright. You are now in mountain pose. Take three deep breaths.

2. Slowly, focusing your attention on your movement, bend over at your waist, dropping your head to the floor. Let the weight of your head fold you over further; let your arms dangle, or you can hold your opposite elbows and rest your head between your arms. You are now in a forward fold pose.

3. Take three deep breaths here, letting your thought bubbles pop as you stay folded.

4. Slowly, curl your body up, one vertebra at a time. Keep breathing and take your time until you are completely upright.

5. Turn your thoughts to your body; focus on how it feels and where there are sensations.

6. Start over again from mountain pose, paying attention to how your body feels as you slowly fold forward, pause, and then curl back upright again.

You can also do a forward fold in a seated position. Sit tall on the floor with your legs straight out in front of you, a slight bend in your knees, with feet together and toes up. As you slowly bend forward at the waist, reach your hands toward your toes. Take a few deep breaths there, paying attention to not straining your back, and if you feel like you're flexible enough, grab your big toes with your index fingers and thumbs to help fold further into your lap. Slowly, curl back up into the seated position, take three deep breaths, and try it again. Yoga is a practice.

Two things the sudden loss of a loved one teaches us are that we can't go back and redo the past, and we don't have control over the future. Yoga, however, teaches us that we do have the ability to focus and put our attention on the present moment—what's happening right now. When it comes to grief, one of the intentions of yoga is to shift your focus from those thought bubbles that put you in the past or future and instead give your mind and body a break. It takes practice, both to master the poses and to let go of thoughts.

Besides helping us pay attention in the moment, the forward fold pose helps move more blood into our brains, giving it more oxygen and kicking our parasympathetic (calming) nervous system into gear. Balancing yoga poses, such as tree pose described below, also help calm our nerves, because while doing them we're focused on paying attention to the ground under us and to maintaining stability and balance, not our anxious, worrisome thoughts.

6.5 Tree Pose

1. Begin in mountain pose.

2. Take a deep breath and place your weight on your right foot, letting your left foot relax and hang out a minute while you focus on solidly planting (remember the triangle points) your right foot. Notice how strong your right foot and leg are as they hold you up.

3. Now shift your attention to your left foot and slowly move it over toward the arch of your right foot. Point your toes toward the floor as if your left foot is a kickstand on your bike. Maintain your balance and weight on your right foot.

4. When you are ready, place your left foot on your right calf so you are standing only on your right leg. Keep breathing as you maintain your balance.

5. Once you feel balanced, you can raise your arms above your head and spread them out a little so your body looks like a fully blossomed tree, or you can hold your hands together in the middle of your chest, at your heart. Keep breathing.

6. If you want to challenge yourself and focus your attention even more, raise your left foot farther up and rest it on the inside of your right thigh. To maintain your balance in this pose, you may want to fix your eyes on something across the room; focusing your attention on one point helps you keep your balance.

7. After a few breaths, gently lower your left leg and shake it out a little; shake out your right leg too. Return to mountain pose and repeat all the steps using the opposite leg.

Tree pose, or any yoga balance pose, will make you feel powerful and strong and *in* your body. Anxiety and fear develop from a lack of power or control. The freeze response is partly about fearing you will be overpowered or overwhelmed, as though you have no control over your situation.

Katie was frozen by the fear of her dad dying, of becoming an orphan with nowhere to live and no one to take care of her. In order to release the frozen response, she needed to feel a sense of her own power over the situation and in her body. Practicing the next activity made her feel powerful again.

6.6 Strong Like a Superhero

For this activity you'll need a sense of humor, an open mind, and a little privacy. This is another one of those "fake it 'til you make it" activities that will get you through tough times. Search the Internet for images of superhero poses—you know, Superman with his hands on his hips or Wonder Woman with her fists raised in front of her. Make copies or hold them in your memory.

1. In a private space, take a deep breath, and when you let it out, pose like that superhero. That's right, strike a superhero pose.

2. Laugh at yourself, and then try it again.

3. Hold the pose for two minutes. Keep breathing.

4. Stand in front of a mirror and check out your superhero stance. Laugh again, but feel the power of the pose too.

5. Try a different pose—be a different superhero. The important thing is to take a stand, hold the pose for at least two minutes, and breathe deeply through it.

Harvard professor Amy Cuddy (2015) studied the effects of this activity and found that we make ourselves smaller when we feel powerless and larger when we feel confident, proud, and powerful—that is, not afraid. She had people who were applying for jobs practice this activity before their interviews. She even recommended they go to the restroom and practice right before their interview began. Her research shows that just two minutes of pretending or faking it can make a difference in how you feel about yourself and how others see you. You not only can fake it to make it, you can fake it to *become* it. The strong like a superhero activity helps us not only feel powerful, as Cuddy's research proves, but it also gives us an opportunity to laugh at ourselves, something Emma didn't realize she needed to do.

This was insanely funny to try. I hadn't laughed this much in a long time; it felt so good to laugh again, especially at myself. I couldn't do it without cracking up, but it did help give me a sense of power. The warrior pose helped me even more.

Maybe pretending to be a superhero isn't cutting it for you, even with a Harvard professor's proof that it works. Try using the warrior pose to build your confidence and power instead.

6.7 Warrior Pose

1. Begin in mountain pose.

2. Spread your legs more than hip-width apart. Turn your left foot out, but keep your right foot pointed straight ahead. Be sure your feet are solidly planted (the triangles in place) on the ground.

3. Raise both arms to shoulder height and straight out from your sides. Be sure to not shrug your shoulders, and keep your fingers together and pointed out.

4. Take a deep breath in, and slowly bend your left knee without extending it over the toes on your left foot. You are in a lunge position and should feel stretching but not pain. You may need to spread your legs farther apart to get a good bend to the lunge without your knee going past your toes.

5. Turn your head, not your body, toward your left arm and focus on your fingers or a point beyond them. Breathe three or four times while holding this position.

6. Now to the other side. Lower your arms. Turn your left foot in to face forward and your right foot out to the side. Raise your arms back up to shoulder height. Keeping your body facing straight ahead, bend your right knee without going past your toes, turn your head to the right, and breathe, focusing on your fingertips or what is just beyond.

7. When you are finished, turn your right foot back to center, drop your arms, bring your legs to mountain pose, and focus your attention on the strength and power of the warrior pose you just did.

These poses and activities should help relieve your anxiety, calm your fears, and give you a sense of power and control when grief anxiety and fear burst into your life. Try to remember that many of your anxious thoughts aren't real—they're just thoughts. However, as grievers, we do know real fear too, such as the fear of another loved one dying or the fear of our own death. Many of our anxieties and fears are about no longer feeling safe and secure.

Creating Safety

It's hard to feel safe when our body's fear response has kicked in, when we know from our grief experience that we are not safe from the hurt, pain, anxiety, and fear caused by losing a loved one. Grief can make us feel insecure, unsafe, or untethered, like a kite blowing in the wind and ready to crash into something and fall to the ground.

Anxiety and fear can leave us feeling like we have lost our way, like we have no map to get us to a place where we can feel safe, relaxed, calm, and at peace again—the way we felt before the death. There are ways to move us out of anxiety and fear to places of safety and calm. In the following activity you'll use a technique called guided imagery to guide yourself through anxiety to the image of a safe, calm place. Any time you need to feel safe and calm, you can bring your mind back to this safe space.

6.8 My Safe Space

Find a space that is quiet and calm, where you can sit or lie down, and take a few deep breaths to relax yourself. You can do this activity on the floor of your room, in a chair, or outside on the grass if that feels relaxing and safe. (You can download the audio version of this activity at http://www.newharbinger.com/38532.)

1. Begin with activity 3.1 (whole body muscle relaxation) from chapter 3, "Your Angry Body."

2. Listen to the downloaded script, which will guide you to your safe, calm place.

3. Allow all your senses to connect to the words, and imagine as many details of this space as you can.

4. As the script comes to an end, roll over on your side if you are lying down, or shift your position if you are seated, and breathe and take in the experience of your safe space for a minute or two before you move again.

Now that you have a safe space to go to when anxious or fearful thoughts occur, you have the power and control to use just one word to bring relaxation and peace. Read through the words of the script below; you may want to record yourself reading it so you are truly guiding your own mind toward safety and calm.

My Safe Space Guided Imagery Script

Sit or lie comfortably in a space where you won't be disturbed. Close your eyes and take three big, deep belly breaths, and as you exhale, notice and allow all the parts of your body to relax. Let the weight of your head and shoulders relax; your chest and stomach should be loose, legs and feet resting comfortably.

Bring to your mind the image of a place you have been before, or imagine a place that is peaceful and relaxing for you. Picture it in your mind. It might be a sandy beach, a spot underneath a tree in your yard, or your bathtub filled with bubbles; maybe it's some other magical place you've read about or where you imagine you would feel safe and calm.

With this image, what do you see? Picture every part of this place. Turn your head, in your mind, all the way around and see this place from all angles. Notice the colors. Are they bright and vibrant? Soft and delicate? Can you see them clearly?

Notice the smells. What do all the things in your safe, calm place smell like? Take a deep breath in and smell. Are there flowers? Do you smell water? Or the earth? Maybe you smell chocolate chip cookies baking?

What do you hear? Take your time and really listen. Can you hear wind in the trees, water dripping, or birds singing?

What can you feel? What sensations are you feeling on your skin? Is the sun shining on your face? Is water splashing at your feet?

Picture all the sights, sounds, smells, and sensations of this place. Take three long, deep belly breaths. Now think of a word that describes and symbolizes this place, just one word, and say it out loud three times slowly. Take three more deep belly breaths, and when you are ready, slowly bring your mind back to the place you are in.

Wrap-Up

Your scared body may freeze when you feel threatened, and your brain may put you in a worry response with anxious thoughts. Being able to pay attention to your body's sensations and your mind's thoughts, to find different ways to feel power and control in order to calm down and feel safe, are important parts of healing from the grief of losing a loved one. Whether it is naming your fears, grounding yourself in the present moment, repeating a six-word mantra, undertaking a round of STOP IT, or saying a word that takes you to your safe space, these tools can help you tame the monster of grief anxiety. Any time you find yourself drifting away from the present moment, getting lost in daydreams that feel like nightmares, worrying about the phone ringing, believing that the spot on your arm is cancer, or losing the sense that anything will be safe or calming again, try one or two or three of the activities in this chapter and find the one that works for you. Take back your power and control—be strong, not frozen with fear.

What's Next?

Grieving, finding relief, and paying attention to your body's reactions and your feelings is a lot of work; all this activity can be exhausting. Grief is exhausting. Your body and brain can get so tired that all you want to do is sleep the day away, hoping you'll wake up and realize that the death of your loved one was just a dream or a nightmare. In the next chapter we'll look at ways to help your tired body get the rest it needs in just the right amounts—not too much and not too little.

chapter 7

your tired body

All I did was sleep—all day. I napped even when I slept twelve or fourteen hours at night. Sleeping seemed to make it all go away, until I woke up.

—Emma

I couldn't get to sleep, thinking about JR's last thoughts, so I'd zone out on video games. They kept my mind off things but kept me up most of the night too.

—Matt

When people are asked to talk about grief, they will often say things like "I'm torn apart," "I'm broken," or "I'm shattered," or they describe it as "walking through molasses," "life in slow motion," or "getting knocked back down as soon as you get up." Grief is emotionally, mentally, and physically exhausting. There are many physical signs and symptoms of grief exhaustion, including slowed movement, muscle aches and pains, loss of hunger (which can lead to weakened muscles and dizziness), headaches, stomachaches, shortness of breath, lack of sleep, and oversleeping. They all take a toll on us.

Getting the right amount of sleep, food, and water, along with moving your body regularly, are key to relieving grief exhaustion. In this chapter we will concentrate on the fatigue and sleep problems people suffer from during grief. It's important to find the balance of the right amount of sleep, especially when you can't fall asleep or all you want to do is sleep. Differentiating between when you are truly resting and caring for your grief-exhausted body and when you are just plain living like a sloth because it keeps you from healing and getting back to life is also important. Sometimes sleep is about what we need to heal, and sometimes it can be an escape from dealing with grief.

Too Many or Too Few Zzzz's?

The average teen is supposed to get between eight and ten hours of sleep per night. This amount will assure that you avoid some of the consequences of not getting enough sleep, which include depression, suicide ideation, obesity, increased drug and alcohol use, drowsy (sleep-drunk) driving accidents, and poor academic performance (Owens 2014). Educators, doctors, and parents are concerned that electronic media use, caffeine consumption, and school start times are preventing teens from getting healthy sleep, and the results of ongoing research may lead to suggestions for appropriate amounts of screen time and caffeine and later start times.

When you're grieving, upsetting thoughts about your loved one who died, worry and anxiety about what's going to happen now, bad dreams, or fear of bad dreams could be causing you to have difficulty sleeping. The effects of lack of sleep, some of which you may have experienced, pile up. Frustration increases, as does irritability, anger, hostility, depression, and negativity. You may become easily and frequently overwhelmed; have big emotional outbursts; and be less friendly, happy, or understanding. Your immune system may grow weaker, causing you to be sick more often, and you get hungrier, so you may eat more.

Too Little Sleep

You may be familiar with the term *insomnia*, which is the inability to fall asleep, having trouble staying asleep, and feeling tired all the time. One that may not be so familiar is *hyposomnia*, which is getting too little sleep. *Hypnophobia*, which may apply to some grieving teens, is the fear of sleep. Hypnophobia may be caused by recurrent nightmares or the fear of being awakened with the news of another loved one's death.

Insomnia, hyposomnia, and hypnophobia get in the way of healing your grieving body. What can you do to get closer to the eight to ten hours of sleep you're supposed to have every night? It starts with a bedtime routine. Doing the same thing every night teaches your body to get tired even when it's not.

TOO-FEW-ZZZ'S BEDTIME ROUTINE

If you are not getting enough sleep, are finding it hard to fall asleep, or are waking up during the night, you can develop a bedtime routine to help you get closer to that eight to ten hours of needed sleep. Here are some suggestions for establishing a routine.

The Room

- Set your room up for sleep; block out as much light as you can and be sure to turn the lighting down low an hour before bed.

- Turn your alarm clock to face away from where you sleep if it has a light on it.

- Keep your room cool; use a fan to move air around.

- Consider buying a white-noise machine, which drowns out other noises that might disturb you.

- Use an eye mask and earplugs if they will help quiet and darken your environment.

Preparation

- Try not to take any naps during the day.

- Decide on what time you are going to go to bed, and keep that time even on the weekends for one month.

- Stop drinking caffeine or energy drinks five hours before your bedtime.

- Stop using electronic devices one hour before going to bed; anything with a light on it will convince your brain that it's time to be awake.

- Read a book for pleasure, but don't study.

- Snuggle up with your pet or listen to soft, soothing music in the hour before your set bedtime.

As soon as you climb into bed, begin with a few long, deep breaths. Consider using activity 3.1 (whole body muscle relaxation) or the script from activity 6.8 (my safe space) to relax and calm yourself. Any time a thought bubble of worry, anxiety, or frustration about not falling asleep pops up, imagine yourself poking the bubble and watching the thought vanish. Every time a thought bubbles up, pop it. Do it over and over. Popping thought bubbles is like counting sheep, but it also helps you realize that your thoughts come and go and that you have some control over them and the amount of anxiety you experience.

Too Much Sleep

If you are concerned that you're sleeping too much—you are in bed more than twelve to fourteen hours several days in a row—or if your family is concerned, you may be suffering from hypersomnia. You might want to have your parent or guardian make you an appointment with a doctor who can check to be sure that something isn't physically causing you to sleep so much. The doctor will assess you for depression to be certain that your emotional exhaustion isn't getting out of control. However, establishing a bedtime routine can also help you get back to an ideal sleep pattern of eight to ten hours of sleep a night.

TOO-MANY-ZZZ'S BEDTIME ROUTINE

Here are some suggestions for establishing a routine when you are sleeping too much.

The Room

- Set your room up for waking. Be sure morning light can filter through the windows.

- Don't use white-noise machines or similar sounds to lull yourself to sleep at night.

- Keep your room temperature a little warmer than usual; getting overheated will wake your body up and move you out of sleep.

Preparation

- Determine what time you are going to go to sleep each night and get up each morning.

- Avoid napping during the day by getting active; as soon as you feel like taking a little snooze, put on some loud party music or go for a walk. Whatever you do, don't sit or lie down; check out activity 4.1 (move) for ideas.

- Avoid caffeine and energy drinks even if you sleep more than you'd like. Energy drinks mess with your *circadian rhythm,* your body's natural clock that says when it's time to go to sleep and to wake up. Moving around, stimulating your senses with music that is energetic, will do just as much as an energy drink— and it won't knock you out of your natural circadian rhythm.

- Try some of the activities discussed later in the chapter to energize your exhausted body when you are fighting sleep. Do them when you feel like taking a nap or as soon as your alarm goes off in the morning and you want to roll over and go back to sleep.

- Tune your alarm clock to play music that will wake you up, and put the clock somewhere across the room so you have to get out of bed to turn it off.

- Place a glass of water next to the alarm clock. Drinking water after you turn off your alarm will help wake you up.

Bedtime Activities

Whether you are getting too many or too few zzz's at night, there are a couple of activities you can add to your bedtime routine that will allow you to tame any concerns you have about sleeping, nightmares, or dreams. These activities will help you fall asleep thinking about the good things in your life.

The first activity is journal writing. Journaling has been shown to have a remarkable effect on emotional stability (Borkin 2014), on healing, and on coping with difficult emotions. Doing this activity right before falling asleep allows you to get off your mind anything that might be getting in the way of your sleep. Similar to activity 6.1 (name it to tame it), this activity allows you to write down what you are feeling and experiencing in your chaotic grief journey in order to right it— that is, get things straight in your head or your heart. Seeing your thoughts on paper, expressing them with an open mind and heart, can produce insight and relief that just may help you sleep and live better.

7.1 Write It to Right It

At a bookstore, office or art supply store, or other retail store, pick out a journal or notebook that speaks to you. This is something you are going to want to keep and look at over and over to see how you were able to get through this very difficult time in your life. While you are at it, find a nice pen that will stay with your journal. Keep your journal and pen in the same place in your room, both for privacy and to make journaling part of your bedtime routine.

1. Begin with your story, as if you were telling it to a new friend for the first time. Start with where you were born and describe who your family is, where you go to school, who your friends are, and so on. Write down everything about yourself. Take as many nights as you need for this step (and all the steps in this exercise).

2. Tell the story of who died, including how, when, your feelings, your thoughts, what you notice in your body, and how it has affected you spiritually. Do you behave differently now? If yes, then write about it.

3. Make a list of all the things you remember about your loved one. They can be big and small things, things from a long time ago, or things from just before she died.

4. Write a letter to your loved one. It can be a letter of forgiveness, a letter of gratitude, a love letter thanking him for being in your life.

5. Make a list of all the things you wish you could tell your loved one, things you wish you would have said or done together. List the things that have happened since this person died.

6. Write about how you are coping with the loss, what your strengths are as you go through your grief, what meaning you have found in life, and any beliefs you have since your loved one died.

Remember, the journal is about your thoughts and your feelings and not simply a school essay or assignment, so make it yours. Draw pictures, doodle, or change up the color of pen you use. Matt found early on that what he chose to draw or write affected his ability to fall asleep.

I didn't write so much in my journal at night as I drew. I drew whatever came to my mind at first. Sometimes those pictures got wicked, so I switched to just drawing what would relax me. I still draw in my "chill-out" book every night.

Matt adjusted the journaling activity to fit his needs, and you can do the same. The point of this activity and those to come, and adjustments to your room and how you approach sleeping, is to establish a routine that will tell your body it needs sleep, and just the right amount. If like Matt you find that "wicked" drawings or thoughts are keeping you awake, you can always get a different journal in which to express them.

After you finish writing in your journal, or doing any activities from this book that relax and calm you, it's important to do the next activity. Researchers studied activity 7.2 (three good things) as an alternative to antidepressant medications and found it to be just as effective at changing brain chemistry and lifting depression (Seligman et al. 2005). After just two weeks of doing this activity, people with diagnosed depression experienced improvements in their emotions and life. Drifting off to sleep thinking of the good things that happened that day is a pretty nice way to lift your mood and get your zzz's. Finding something good in each day will help you and your body recover from grief and live a fuller, happier life that honors your loved one.

7.2 Three Good Things

Do this activity after you've done any of the activities in the book that relax you, after you've practiced popping some of those thought bubbles, after you've been in bed a little while, or just before you are ready to doze off.

1. Take three deep breaths.

2. Without a lot of thinking, remember three good things that happened during the day. These things don't have to be big, great, amazing, wonderful things, just good things. Maybe you had a really good dinner or a talk with a friend, both of which are good things. Maybe you passed a test you were worried about or just went to school all day without crying—another good thing. Maybe you felt normal or smiled a real smile today—a good thing.

3. Let your mind wander and relax as you remember three good things.

4. Keep taking deep breaths as you drift off to sleep.

Exhaustion Overload or Sloth-Like Indifference?

Too little or too much sleep isn't the only struggle your tired, grieving body goes through. You may also experience fatigue, which is different from being drowsy and ready for sleep. *Fatigue* is a lack of energy and motivation; you are tired all the time and feel weary and indifferent, and the things you once enjoyed seem like more than you can handle. Katie describes fatigue well:

I didn't have the energy to do anything—didn't even want to call my friends. Everything felt like too much work. I just didn't care.

When considering whether or not you're experiencing fatigue, it's important to ask yourself whether or not the fatigue is related to your grief or if it's just a way to perpetuate a habit you've gotten into. Are you avoiding your feelings and giving yourself a reason to not heal your grief? Are you actually experiencing grief fatigue, or are you comfortable being a sloth because it allows you to avoid moving forward in your life? These are tough questions to ask yourself, but you need to.

Teens are often surprised by the feelings of exhaustion and fatigue that come with grief, when pumping caffeine into their body doesn't seem to give them energy. When you're feeling fatigued, physically drained, there are a number of ways to boost your energy in the moment without slamming down an energy drink. These activities will increase your energy for longer periods and cost less!

7.3 Energy Boosters

These activities are quick and easy, and you can do them just about anywhere. They will boost your energy to get you through your next class, your homework, or one of those long and silent family meals.

Pat down to wake up. Hold one of your arms out in front of you, palm side up. Use your other hand to pat your open arm from armpit to wrist. Turn your arm around and pat from the shoulder to the back of the hand. Repeat with the other arm. You can pat the fronts of your legs too.

Earlobe rubdown. Using your index finger and thumb on both hands, rub your ears. Start at the tops of your ears next to the skull and rub down to your earlobes. Then start at your earlobes and rub up to the tops of your ears. Repeat this two more times.

Stand up. That's it. Just stand up. Because your legs need energy to hold the weight of you, your body creates more energy when you stand. The more often and longer you stand, the more energy your body generates. Standing lets your chest be open for bigger, deeper breaths, giving you more oxygen, which also gives you more energy. The next time you play a video game or binge-watch something, lift up the screen and stand in front of it.

Lemon lift. The smell of lemon wakes up your senses and triggers your brain to activity. The smell of lemon can also boost your mood, or try squeezing lemon juice right into your mouth; that will pucker you up and wake you up!

Go outside. When you are outside, pay attention to what is happening around you. Put away your phone and listen to the sounds; smell your surroundings and try to identify the scents. Look closely at an object and see if you notice something different in your everyday environment: check to see if the neighbor finally put away his holiday decorations or pay attention to the seasonal changes in a particular tree.

YouTube energy. You may get a boost of energy by watching silly YouTube videos. Search for funny cats, people laughing, or people falling down. This may be the least effective method, but it's worth a try.

The Comfort in Grief

The physical, mental, and emotional exhaustion in grief are real. They not only affect your body in the short term but can alter your long-term energy levels as well. If you have seen a doctor, don't have a diagnosis of depression, and have tried all of the above activities and *still* feel like nothing has helped, it may be time to take a look at whether you have gotten comfortable in your grief.

What? How could anyone get comfortable in grief? For some people the exhaustion and fatigue of grief become a way of being that is easier to live with than facing the work of moving through grief and toward living life again. Others identify themselves by their grief—"This is who I am now, the girl whose mom died. I'm supposed to be exhausted and sad all the time." Others may have appreciated the comfort they received from people, so they get comfortable in their grief.

Take a minute and think about how or if any of this relates to you. Write about it in your journal or talk to your friends about whether or not they see you getting comfortable in your grief, or whether or not you're identifying yourself as a griever rather than as grieving. Are you settling in to this grief way of being? Do you introduce yourself in conversations as "My dad died and I cry every day"? Are you using your grief as an excuse to sleep in and skip school on days you don't want to go anyway? There's a fine line between the healthy expression of grief (feeling your feelings, having good and bad days, knowing you'll be having more good days than bad in the future) and finding comfort in grief (identifying as a griever first, allowing yourself the luxury of sloth-like living, using grief as your reason why).

If you recognize yourself in any of the descriptions of what it means to be comfortable in your grief, you're not alone. Responding to grief in these ways is common for teens, but they are not very healthy ways. Being aware of these types of responses is the best way to make changes. Perhaps you don't know of any other way to get your emotional needs met. You might want to talk it through with a caring and supportive adult or good friend. Remember, getting out of your comfort zone is always hard.

Wrap-Up

Sleep changes and exhaustion are part of healing from grief, and they are part of your normal teenage growth and development. Remember the importance of establishing routine in order to get your body to know what it needs. Your world (your brain and your body) was turned upside down with the death of your loved one; getting things back to normal or routine will help you heal and grow through your grief.

Moving through exhaustion and getting energy back in your body naturally will prevent depression from settling in, complicating your grief and your life even more. Allow yourself days of sloth-like behavior, but be sure to have days when you work on increasing your level of energy. If you're feeling exhausted, make a point of busting through the list of energy boosters (activity 7.3) as often as you can throughout the day, and please adjust any of the activities in this chapter or this book to fit your individual needs. You and your body will be glad you did.

What's Next?

Getting sick, catching the flu or a cold, is so much easier when you are grieving. Your body's immune system slows down when you are in shock after the death of a loved one. In the next chapter we'll explore how to avoid overloading your already grieving body with illness.

chapter 8

your sick body

I really thought I had cancer too. Everyone always said I was just like my mother, and I started to get the same kind of symptoms that she had, feeling sick all the time, skin rashes; my hair even started falling out.

—Katie

It's not surprising that Katie thought she might have cancer after her mother died from the same disease. Even though you know you can't catch cancer or any other life-threatening disease like you catch a cold, it still feels like you could. And once you start feeling sick with stomachaches, headaches, skin rashes, and so forth, it's not a big leap to being afraid that you have a deadly disease.

We've talked a lot about how stress affects our brain, initiating the fight, flight, freeze, faint response, which then increases the amount of stress hormones in the body in order to carry out the response behaviors. When our body is chronically stressed, our muscles are bathed in stress hormones and our body exhausts itself and starts to break down. In other words, stress literally makes us sick.

In this chapter we'll talk about how our body can get sick from grief and what to do to get healthy again. The first step is not ignoring symptoms. Katie needed to see her family doctor right away and let him know what she was feeling. Trying to feel better when you always feel bad can lead to substance abuse, so we'll address what to do if you find yourself drinking or using drugs to dull the pain. We'll talk about how the anniversary of the death of a loved one can suppress your immune system and make you sick just when you thought things were getting better. And finally, we'll look at some ways to honor and remember your loved one on those anniversary days.

Understanding How Grief Can Make You Sick

We know that when we first hear the news of a loved one's death, our body automatically responds with the stress response, which increases the level of stress hormones (cortisol and adrenaline) in our body ten to twenty times more than usual. Over time, say months of grieving, these high levels of stress hormones wear down our immune system.

The immune system, made up of white blood cells, is meant to fight off unwanted, unhealthy cells in the body. When white blood cells notice something is "off," they take charge and override the predator, or sick, cell. The immune system views stress hormones as sick cells, and fighting them over and over, day after day, leaves the immune system weakened, giving your body little defense to fight disease.

Over time, elevated levels of stress hormones in your body can lead to headaches, migraines, stomachaches, nausea, diarrhea, constipation, muscle aches, back and neck pain, dizziness, shakiness, trembling, dry mouth, shortness of breath, chest pain, unusual skin rashes, chills, sweating, clumsiness, flu-like symptoms, cold symptoms, increased acne, and obesity. Add to this list the exhaustion discussed in the previous chapter, or the broken heart syndrome discussed in chapter 5, and it's easy to see how we can become *sick with grief*. Knowing how grief affects the body can help us make changes to heal it.

I'm Sick—Now What?

Once we know better—how the stress of grief affects the body and immune system—we can do better. There are things you can do immediately to reduce the stress in your body and life in order to get healthier.

Getting healthier, more nutritious foods into your body will give it the energy it needs to fight illness. I'm talking about green vegetables, fruits, plenty of protein, and tons of water—as much water as you can drink! A healthy diet will make a big difference in how you feel and how often you get sick. Getting eight to ten hours of sleep will also give your muscles a chance to settle down and release some stress. Practicing stress-reduction activities, such as mindfulness or guided imagery, and exercising outdoors will also keep your body healthy. However, if you've tried all these things and still feel sick, try the following activity.

8.1 Sick of Grief

1. Make a doctor's appointment and keep it.

2. For seven days before your appointment, pay attention to your body. Focus on any aches and pains. Is your right knee sore? Do you have a hard time breathing going up the steps? Do you want to throw up after every meal? Or maybe just breakfast?

3. Every time you notice something in your body, write it down. Be sure you note where on or in your body you felt it, for how long, and what time of day or night. Did you notice the pain change after a meal? If so, what did you eat? Get as much detail as you can.

4. List the top three things that seem to bother you the most and the most often, are the most painful or the most noticeable, and really mess things up for you during the day.

5. Take the list of three things to your doctor's appointment and ask for an explanation for why you may be feeling this way. You're looking for reasons *why*, not just a way to fix the problems. Be sure to let the doctor know that you are grieving.

6. Also be sure to let the doctor know what you have been doing to prevent illness. Have you been eating healthy food, getting rest, drinking plenty of water, and exercising but still don't feel well?

7. Follow your doctor's recommendations. Make a follow-up appointment for six weeks later.

It's important to be very specific about your health concerns when you see your doctor and to follow her orders for how to get healthier. Making a follow-up appointment will help you be sure to continue to track your symptoms and note if your health is improving.

Most doctors will recognize that grief has caused increased stress and advise you on ways to reduce it, including talking with someone about your grief. One of the most helpful things you can do for grief, and ultimately your physical well-being, is to take care of your emotional well-being. What helps you express your emotions? Who can you talk to about your stress, your grief, and your pain? As we talked about in chapter 4, suppressing emotions will not help your body relieve stress, and ultimately it will lead you to more physical illness and emotional pain.

Relieving stress through whatever means you enjoy and are able to do often is an important way to heal your body and prevent it from getting sick. This book includes a number of ideas and activities designed specifically for stress reduction. Here is one of my favorites.

8.2 Healing My Hurt

Find a safe, quiet, and calm place to relax and listen to this guided imagery activity whenever you feel unhealthy or worried that you're getting sick. (You can download the audio version of this activity at http://www.newharbingor .com/38532.)

1. Take three deep breaths. Let your body sink into the chair, into the couch, or onto the floor with each breath.

2. Relax your legs and your arms; let your hands fall open and be relaxed. Loosen your shoulders, jaw, and brow as you continue to breath normally.

3. As you begin to listen to the guided imagery script, focus your attention on the area of your body that is sick or hurting the most right now.

Healing My Hurt Guided Imagery Script

With each breath you take, imagine you inhale healing and exhale hurt and pain. Inhale health and well-being, exhale sickness. Inhale light and comfort, exhale darkness and disease.

Draw your attention now to the area of your body that feels pain, hurt, illness, or discomfort. As you breathe in, imagine you are bringing a warm, yellow light to this area, and as you breathe out, imagine the pain, hurt, illness, or discomfort breaking into smaller pieces. Keep breathing in the warm, yellow light of healing and breathing out the pieces of your pain and illness until there are no more pieces to exhale.

Breathe in this warm, yellow light of healing to any other parts of your body that need healing and comfort right now.

As you take your next breath, imagine the healing light entering your body from the top of your head and slowly, warmly, moving its yellow light throughout your body. See and feel the light wash over your forehead, your eyes, your jaw, and your neck. Pay attention as the light moves across your shoulders, down your arms, and across your chest. Let the light rest at your heart for as long as your heart needs the warm, healing comfort. Let the light move through your stomach, down your legs, and over the bottoms of your feet before making its way up your back. When you get to your heart, let the light rest there. Take three deep breaths, and tell yourself, *May I be well, may I be healthy, may I be comforted by the healing light of my own heart.*

Katie found comfort in this activity as she awaited the results of a six-week follow-up with her doctor. It helped relieve not only her pain but also the fear and anxiety she felt wondering what illness she might have.

148

Sometimes the emotional and physical pain of grief are so overwhelming that all we want is immediate relief. Eating and sleeping well may not seem possible. After a while, everyone you want to talk to about your pain has already heard it, and they want you to move on. Maybe the activities in this book seem like too much work. You just want something that will make it all go away—a magic pill or potion. Some teens see substance use as the magic that will take away all the hurt. However, there is no magic to take away your grief, and substance use will pile more hurt on top of what's already there.

Dopamine, Drugs, and Drinking

Any addictive substance—drugs, alcohol, or food—meant to take away feelings only distorts and interferes with them. Drowning your grief and feelings in alcohol or drugs will not take them away. They always float back up.

Any substance that makes us feel good is triggering the dopamine responders in our brain. Dopamine is the reward chemical that sends signals throughout our body saying *This feels good. Do it again!* The more we use a substance, the more we need to feel that way, and because our body and brain develop a tolerance to its effects, we have to use more of the substance or a different substance altogether. Matt found that beer wasn't making him feel good enough anymore, so he moved on to smoking weed. Neither took away the grief, but they temporarily masked it.

One night I just couldn't stop; it started out okay, just having some fun, but then someone brought up JR's name and I downed a few beers to deal with that. They didn't help. So I smoked some pot, drank a few more beers, and I guess I blacked out. Nothing scarier than waking up not knowing where you are or what happened—nothing.

Matt is not alone in this experience. Research has shown that 50 percent of teens who had a traumatic loss abused substances (Institute for Trauma and Stress at the NYU Child Study Center 2002). Matt found himself using more and different substances with little change in his feelings of grief; he realized he was paying a bigger price for trying to feel good with drugs and alcohol.

Matt was motivated to make changes after his blackout, but he wasn't sure where to start. He didn't think he needed treatment, but after talking with an adult he trusted, he did get an assessment for drug and alcohol abuse from a mental health professional. Matt knew he wanted to change how he was coping with his grief, especially his drinking and drugging. The question was where to start. Here's what he did to get back on track.

8.3 Thirty-Day Plan to Change

You need a pencil and about an hour of quiet time alone. Use the form available at http://www.newharbinger.com/38532, and follow the steps to change things in your life that aren't working, don't feel good, or make your life miserable.

1. Take three deep breaths.

2. List one to three things you plan to change in the next thirty days. Be specific, positive, and realistic about the changes you want to make.

3. Consider why you want to make each of these changes. What's motivating you? What are the consequences if you don't change?

4. Now list your plan. What are the steps you'll need to take to make this change? When or how will these steps need to be done? Set dates; remember, you have thirty days to complete the changes.

5. We need others to help us make changes or to encourage us while we change. Who are the people who will support you?

6. Now list specifically how they can help you, and how you will ask for their support.

7. What might go wrong? What could get in your way? If you know what may block your change, you can go around it.

8. Picture the change happening: list what it looks like, what's different, and what benefits you are seeing from the change. What will it be like for you in thirty days?

9. Once you have completed the thirty-day plan to change form, post it somewhere you can see it every day.

10. Set your plan in motion. Each day, revisit the plan and check off or scratch out what you have accomplished. If you journal, this is a great activity to write about on each of the thirty days.

11. Though the satisfaction of planning for and making changes happen in your life is reward in and of itself, once you have experienced some success, get yourself through the remaining days of your thirty-day plan by planning (around day twenty-one) your completion celebration.

The thirty-day plan to change is a great way to shift your focus from wanting to feel good with drugs and drinking to working toward real change that will make you feel good for longer than a Saturday-night party. Matt found he could start with just one change, and, without noticing it, other changes happened automatically.

I thought I'd take it one change at a time on this one, so
I just chose to change my drinking—to stop for thirty days.
Turns out I stopped smoking too in those thirty days.
The next thirty-day plan for change was to find a way
to remember JR that meant something.

When people are stressed out day after day, they make poor choices to relieve stress. Whether it is drinking, drugging, smoking, eating junk food, playing video games, binge-watching TV, using social media excessively, or shopping, these short-term addictive behaviors will not ease your stress or pain long term. Here is a list of more ways to get that feel-good dopamine charge without resorting to addictive behaviors.

8.4 Fifty Things That Feel Good

1. Walk the dog.
2. Pet the cat.
3. Volunteer at an animal shelter.
4. Call your best friend.
5. Reread a good book.
6. See a funny movie.
7. Ride a bike.
8. Go for a swing.
9. Go for a swim.
10. Plan a trip anywhere in the world.
11. Go to a museum, the library, a record store, or an antique shop.
12. Read to a child.
13. Have a dance party for one.
14. Donate something.
15. Find five cloud animals.
16. Be kind to someone without him or her knowing.
17. Go to the beach.
18. Plant flowers somewhere.
19. Make art.
20. Watch the sun set all the way.
21. Send a thank-you note to someone.
22. Surprise someone.
23. Make a bucket list.
24. Shoot hoops.
25. Take a bubble bath.
26. Build a fort.
27. Stargaze.
28. Read, or better yet write, a poem.
29. Fly a kite.
30. Play Frisbee.
31. Sing into your hairbrush.
32. Visit the zoo.
33. Smile at five people.
34. Splash in the rain.
35. Color with crayons.
36. Drink a glass of lemon water.
37. Kiss someone.
38. Smell flowers.
39. Finish a one-thousand-piece puzzle.
40. Hold a baby—a baby anything.
41–50. Make a list of ten things that make you feel good.

Listing things that feel good is a way to start feeling better, to stay healthy, and to honor your feelings and grief. Feeling good doesn't mean your grief goes away. Grief will be with you as long as you remember the person who died. You'll have days when you feel good all day, realizing you didn't feel sad or mad or anxious or worried once the whole day. And then the grief will be back—a wave of sadness, more tears, a burst of anger that your loved one isn't here and she should be. Birthdays, holidays, and the anniversary of the day your loved one died are typically days when you will notice this person's absence.

Anniversary Grief

When someone you love dies, the calendar of your life is changed forever. There is a new date to remember, the anniversary, and time becomes *before* the person died and *after*. For some people, the anniversary is the actual day their loved one died; for others, the anniversary can be the kind of day it was when their loved one died, such as a cold, dark winter day or a beautiful, sunny Saturday. And when the anniversary day or one of these similar days rolls around, grief surges back up. This is called anniversary grief. Emma's grief was tied to a season.

> *As soon as the weather got nice, the sun was warm, and the grass started turning green, all the sadness came back, and my brother's anger. Everyone else was ready for summer vacations, the beach and happy times... Not us.*

Anniversary grief is easier to deal with once you know about it. For so many people who are grieving for the first time, it can come as a surprise. You question what is wrong with yourself, because you were doing so well. What brought on this sudden surge of pain and grief? Then you might look at the calendar and realize that a whole year has passed since your loved one died. Or maybe you dread the anniversary date so much you have a month or a season of grief—all day, every day. Sometimes anniversary grief creeps up on you; instead of a date on the calendar, it is the first subzero day in January, when the snow cracks and every breath surrounds your face with steam, because that was how cold it was the day you found out. Our memories are stored with our senses; our senses, especially our sense of smell, usually get triggered before our thoughts realize what the date is.

If not expressed, anniversary grief can make you sick. Trying not to think about or acknowledge the anniversary can backfire. Many grieving people report getting sick around the time of the anniversary, whether in anticipation of the day or wanting to avoid it altogether; our body seems to remember. To avoid getting sick, you can plan for or anticipate what you will do to recognize that day. Even if your plan is to spend the day curled up in bed with a box of tissues, preparing for the feelings the anniversary brings and finding a way to express your feelings will keep you healthier, both physically and emotionally.

Many people establish a ritual or tradition on the anniversary day to acknowledge and remember their loved one and to celebrate having made it through the past year, the past two years, or the past five years. Survivors often find an activity to give their grief meaning on anniversary days, such as releasing balloons, lighting a candle, or looking at photos. What's important is finding a way to remember that works for you.

8.5 Remembering-You Space

Locate a small space somewhere out of the way but visible, such as a table next to your bed, the top of your dresser, or a shelf in your closet. Gather mementos of your loved one, such as a photograph, something that was special to him, or a piece of his clothing.

1. Play music that is soothing or reminds you of your loved one.

2. Take three deep breaths and focus your attention on your loved one.

3. Clear off and clean up the space and put down a nice cloth or a piece of clothing that belonged to your loved one.

4. Place a photograph of your loved one in this space. Take a minute to pause and remember where the photo was taken. What was happening that day?

5. At any time leading up to the anniversary, feel free to add whatever reminds you of your loved one, pausing to remember him as you do so. Take three deep breaths before and after placing something special in the remembering-you space.

6. Finally, add a candle, a wind chime, or a special religious symbol to the space on the anniversary day.

On the anniversary of Sophie's death, Emma's family chose to decorate the swing set and slide in their backyard with ribbons of her favorite color, and they planted a flower garden around them. They began a tradition of growing and releasing butterflies each summer to remind them of Sophie. With each anniversary, more and more people from the neighborhood began participating, and now they release over one hundred butterflies at the beginning of every summer. Memorializing Sophie in these ways changed Emma's relationship with anniversary grief.

I never thought I would ever like summer again. I thought summer would always remind me of how sad life is; instead, now I look forward to butterfly-release day, with all the squeals and sighs. So weird and so cool to see my big brother, the big green monster who tore the door off his bedroom, gently holding a butterfly on his finger, launching it into the sky, right there by Sophie's slide. There are still tears and lots of hugs, but we're mostly happy now when summer arrives.

Finding ways to remember our loved ones, to feel good without using substances, and to keep our body healthy and well while experiencing grief is possible. Sometimes these practices can even bring happiness back.

Wrap-Up

When we're stressed, when our lives get turned upside down, and when we're grieving, it is very easy to make poor choices that affect our health. Grieving makes it harder to sleep, to eat well, and to want to get exercise. Grieving alters our body and brain chemistry, suppressing our immune system and causing us to get sick more often. Trying to feel good through addictive behaviors, such as drinking and drugging, only further taxes our body and prolongs the inevitable pain of grief, and the results of these behaviors only make life worse.

Our lives were changed by the loss of a loved one, and change is hard. With a plan to change for the better, to feel good again without drugs or drinking, and to avoid getting sick over and over again, some of the hurt and pain of loss can be eased. For starters, getting enough rest, healthy food, and exercise will help keep you healthy, and planning for the anniversary of your loss, finding the space and time to remember and honor your loved one, will also help you feel better emotionally and physically.

What's Next?

In the next chapter we'll explore ways to calm yourself. These practices will not only relieve grief, they will help you get through life's other tests, big and small—a calculus exam, your driver's license test, a broken relationship, marriage, the birth of a baby, a major illness, or the death of someone else you love. Learning the skills to calm your body during grief and times of illness or stress is a gift that will last a lifetime.

chapter 9

your calm body

I would get so worked up trying to figure out why JR did this, how I could have prevented it, what life would be like without him. Everyone kept telling me to calm down, relax, but no one told me how I was supposed to do that.

—Matt

Finding a way to stay calm in the midst of a grief storm is not easy. Many of the activities you've learned so far have a foundation in calming the body down, but this chapter will highlight some of the reasons why the body wants a calm state and ways to get there when life turns chaotic.

Our body is meant to fire up when we are presented with stressful situations, but our body is also made to calm down. Do you remember that our brains contain the autonomic nervous systems with the sympathetic (fire up) and parasympathetic (calm down) parts? We often can't predict or control the firing up, but we do have the ability to self-soothe. The activities in this chapter will help you with that.

Just Relax

Whenever we tell someone we are stressed or someone sees that we are experiencing the fight, flight, freeze, faint response, we're often told to "just relax"—as if it were that easy. Though it may not seem so at the time, there is some sense behind this advice.

Way back in 1974, a Harvard heart doctor named Herbert Benson (Benson et al. 1974) developed what he calls the *relaxation response*, which is a way to respond to the fight, flight, freeze, faint mode and its effects on the body. His research shows that this response supports the hypothalamus in the brain. The hypothalamus is responsible for keeping brain chemicals and hormones balanced. When the amygdala, the brain's fire alarm, is fired up from stress or a threat, the hypothalamus soothes and calms it down. Benson's relaxation response is meant to keep the hypothalamus working efficiently enough during times of stress to calm us down. There are many ways to bring about the relaxation response, including the following activity.

9.1 Body Scan

Find a comfortable place to sit or lie down. Be sure to wear comfortable clothing, and take off your shoes. (You can download the audio version of this activity at http://www.newharbinger.com/38532.)

1. Take three deep breaths.

2. You can close your eyes or let them fall out of focus.

3. Begin checking in with your whole body and getting comfortable. What is your position? Is there tension or tightness anywhere?

What are your feelings and emotions right now? Is your mind busy, focused, anxious, or calm? Don't have any judgments, just notice and be aware of these things. There is no right or wrong answer to this.

4.   Focus on your breath. Where is the breath in your body? Is it in your chest, stomach, or throat? Notice where the breath comes in and goes out of your body. Can you envision your lungs and your heart as part of your breath or the start of your breath?

5.   Notice the bottom of your body, starting with your toes or the bottoms of your feet. Notice the sensations in each part of your body. Notice if there is tingling, heaviness, lightness, itchiness, warmth, or coolness. Is there a pressure or pulsing? Be aware of these feelings or sensations and just be curious about them; there is nothing to do with them but notice. Be aware of all parts of your feet: bottoms, tops, and ankles.

6.   Move up into your legs, noticing your calves, shins, knees, thighs, and hamstrings…your whole leg. Let your mind feel both of your legs. If you notice no specific feeling, notice and be curious about that. Keep breathing.

7.   Now shift your attention to your hips. Notice how you can move your attention to your body and not have to do anything. Just let the sensations that are there be there.

8.   Pay attention as you move your attention to your torso—your back, your chest, your stomach, and your ribs…breathing in and out. This region of the body holds many emotions, so spend a few minutes paying attention and feeling what is in the torso, letting whatever is there just be.

9. Shift attention from the torso to the arms, wrists, and hands down to the tips of your fingers. Slowly move your attention to each area of your arms and hands.

10. Move up to the neck and throat. What is there as you breathe in and out? Notice with curiosity.

11. Slide your attention up to your face, your mouth, nose, ears, eyes, and forehead. Scan your entire face and notice the sensations that are there as you continue to breathe in and out.

12. Now move your attention and your breath across the top of your head, down the sides of your scalp, and to the back of your head. What do you notice? Do you feel the point where your head rests on the pillow or floor? Is there a feeling of heaviness as you sit holding your head up?

13. Keep breathing in and out and scan your entire body now, letting go of the attention you placed on your scalp, face, neck, arms, torso, hips, legs, and feet; feel your body as a whole, gently focusing your attention now on your breath. Feel your body...connected and whole...as you feel your breath go in...and out.

14. End this practice by noticing the calm nature of your body, in its individual parts and as a whole. Breathe in calm...breathe out calm.

The body scan is a mindfulness meditation practice that will help you notice and be aware of what your body is doing and feeling in any given moment. To be mindful of body sensations, to be embodied, is a practice that will help you calm yourself when you are anxious or when anxiety-producing things happen. Matt found the body scan useful several times in his life.

After getting used to the body scan routine, I found I could just relax whenever I needed to. I even did it in class a few times; nobody knew. After a while, people stopped trying to get me to just relax.

You don't have to do the body scan lying down; it's more calming that way, but it is still effective whenever and however you practice it. The body scan is a way to stay connected to your body, to own your body, and to know it in a way that can help you recognize and prevent mental and physical illness well into your adult years. Get in the habit of doing a body scan regularly; your health and well-being will be better for it.

Your body and brain, as you've learned, are made up of processes, systems, and chemicals that, once understood, can make you healthy or cause illness. It's helpful to already understand the chemistry involved in calming your anxious and grieving body when searching for ways to deal with chaos or the crises of life.

Chemicals of Calm

The body naturally produces calming chemicals in your brain. The main calming chemicals are serotonin and GABA. Though they are naturally produced, we can provide our body and brain with additional serotonin and GABA through food and supplements.

Serotonin is the brain chemical affected by antidepressant drugs. Serotonin affects our mood and ability to maintain calm, but it also can affect sleep, appetite, impulse control, and sexual desire. Serotonin offsets the effects of the stress hormone cortisol in the brain. Tryptophan, another natural chemical in the body, helps produce serotonin. Whole-grain foods (such as whole wheat bread or brown rice), turkey, and bananas are a great source of tryptophan; eating them will increase the levels of serotonin in your body (Benton and Donohoe 1999). Another effective way to get more serotonin is to use supplements. Nutrition or health-food stores sell serotonin-enhancing supplements called 5-HTP, or 5-hydroxytryptophan.

GABA, or gamma-aminobutyric acid, is another naturally occurring brain chemical. It works with serotonin to calm down and balance the chemicals in the brain. You can take GABA as an over-the-counter supplement or try valerian root or the amino acid L-theanine to boost your GABA levels. You can find all of these supplements at your local health-food store.

Making "Scents" of Calm

As we learned in chapter 2, our sense of smell is activated in the fight, flight, freeze, faint response, and we can use our sense of smell to calm ourselves when we are agitated or shift into this mode. Native Americans have used scents to alter mood and heal emotional states for centuries, and Western healers and health care workers have discovered their benefits more recently. Using scents as a complementary method of healing is called *aromatherapy*. People practice aromatherapy by inhaling the scent of a few drops of an essential oil or combination of oils, or the oils are combined with water and misted into the environment. It is not known what mechanism in the brain these aromas affect; however, because aromatherapy is gaining popularity, at some point research will determine what and why it helps calm people.

One big aromatherapy study (Lehrner et al. 2005) used a dental office as the laboratory. The researchers misted the waiting room with lavender and orange oils. Their study shows that the "misted" dental patients had less anxiety, a higher state of calm, and a generally more positive mood compared with patients who didn't get misted. More and more mental health therapists are using aromatherapy to relax and calm their clients during session. Emma was skeptical at first, but wanting relief, she was willing to give aromatherapy a try.

When my therapist suggested I try smelling lavender to calm my sobbing cryfest, I thought she was nuts. Turns out it really did make me feel better. Now I use it any time I'm feeling a little anxious or stressed out, like right before a big test.

9.2 Lavender Rest

Buy a small bottle of lavender essential oil and an empty spray bottle or cotton balls. Just before going to sleep, or when you need a rest during the day, do the following.

1. Place five to six drops of lavender oil on a cotton ball or in the spray bottle you've filled halfway with water.

2. Lightly spray or mist your pillow with the lavender-oil mixture or place the cotton ball inside your pillow case.

3. Lay on your side, placing your head on the pillow.

4. Take three long, deep breaths, inhaling the scent of the lavender.

5. Relax and rest your body and your mind, inhaling deeply the lavender scent until you feel your body is calm.

To further the sense of calm with lavender scent, try combining this activity with activity 6.8 (my safe space). When you've completed the steps of activity 6.8, place your palms together at the heart level of your chest and rapidly rub them together back and forth several times, creating heat. Gently place your palms over your face with your fingertips above your eyebrows, your thumbs at your cheekbones, and the heels of your palms near your jawline. Your hands should just barely touch these areas of your face. Feel the warmth of your hands surrounding your face. Relax your forehead, your eyes, your jawbone, your mouth, and your teeth. Rest the tip of your tongue on the roof of your mouth. Relax into the moment until you are ready to slowly open your eyes, seeing first through your fingers as you adjust to the light.

Calming Your Body with Mindfulness

Our body and mind are one. Our mind is not just housed inside our brain inside our body; rather, there is a connection between our mind—what we understand, what we know, what we feel—and our body, even if we don't understand fully how they are connected. The more we learn about how the body and the mind work together, especially when we are suffering, the more ability we have to heal both.

You have learned several activities to help you pay attention and notice the sensations in your body. You have learned how the body and the brain are affected by traumatic events, such as the loss of someone you love. Let's now talk about how the mind can become more aware and connected to the body through the ancient practice of mindfulness meditation.

Mindfulness meditation is the practice of setting aside time to become aware of the present moment, noticing your feelings, thoughts, body sensations, and surroundings with a sense of curiosity and acceptance without judgment of whether they are right or wrong. Mindfulness meditation is accepting what is, in this moment. It is a practice and will always be a practice. There is no "winning" at mindfulness, there is just "being" mindful.

Katie practiced mindfulness meditation when she found herself feeling "bad most of the time" and "always thinking bad thoughts" that just kept making her sadder. Practicing mindfulness meditation can help you *see* and *let go* of thoughts and feelings that are about the past or the future, bringing a calm to what is happening right now. Try it for yourself and see what Katie and thousands upon thousands of other grieving people have found helpful in calming their bodies and minds.

9.3 Mindfulness Meditation

Find a quiet spot, without distraction. (If you created a remembering-you space, activity 8.5, sitting in front of this might be helpful.) Using a timer of some sort is helpful with mindfulness meditation; start with just ten minutes, and be sure the volume of the timer alarm is not too loud. (You can download the audio version of this activity at http://www.newharbinger.com/38532.)

1. Sit comfortably, either cross-legged on the floor (with a pillow if you like) or on a chair.

2. Sit as if you were royalty on a throne, proud and upright; honor your body and this practice with that mind-set. To do this, imagine a string or thread beginning at your tailbone, winding through your spine and neck, passing through the top of your head, and attaching to the ceiling. This is just to give you the image of a straight back, erect head, and slightly tucked chin. Pay attention to this

body position, but don't rigidly hold your body in this position; you want to feel comfortable and royal.

3. Sitting this way with mindfulness allows your chest to open and gives your belly room to expand as you breathe comfortably throughout the practice.

4. Rest your hands in your lap, palms up, or set them gently on your knees. If you are seated, be sure your feet are flat on the ground, pointed forward as if on skis.

5. Soften the focus of your eyes by closing your lids just slightly and looking downward. You can also find a focus for your gaze, such as a candle, a photograph, or a memento. Take three deep breaths.

6. Now relax into a normal breathing pattern, noticing your breath go in and out of your body.

7. You can continue to focus your attention on your breath throughout the process, but you may notice your mind start to wander...

8. Thoughts may come up... *This is weird. Am I doing this right? What's supposed to happen? I'm uncomfortable. This is boring!* Let the thoughts bubble up—*That was dumb. I'm not doing this right*—and then don't think about them anymore. Just let the thoughts pass by until the next thought bubbles up.

9. They may be uncomfortable thoughts... *I miss my mom. I wish I could see him again. I wonder what will happen on her birthday.* Just notice them and let them ease on by, out of your mind, as you bring your focus back to this moment.

10. Feelings may come up, tears may flow, your nose may itch. (It's okay to scratch it; mindfulness is not the same as being a robot!) Let yourself notice the feelings and sensations come...and go.

11. Continue to sit, occasionally adjusting your posture to be sure you are sitting with intention, allowing your body to hold itself in a position that eases your breath and keeps your chest open. Notice if you are slumped over, curving your back, or curling your shoulders, and then make the necessary corrections. Again, don't become rigid or "come to attention" like a soldier, but instead be in attention like a king or queen.

12. Sometimes it will feel like it takes forever for the time to pass, and at other times it seems like the timer goes off instantly. When the timer does go off, turn it off and take three deep breaths.

Mindfulness meditation is a simple, but not easy, practice. Again, mindfulness meditation is a practice of connecting your body, your mind, your feelings, and your thoughts with what is happening in the moment, not worrying about the future or thinking about the past. Please don't try it only once and decide it doesn't work or you don't like it or you can't do it. I invite you to take a seven-day challenge: do this activity every day for seven days and see how you feel. After that, challenge yourself to another fourteen days of practice, or thirty days, before you decide whether or not it's for you.

If you do thirty days of mindfulness meditation, you will see a difference. You will find yourself calmer, less anxious, and less stressed; you will be able to concentrate for longer periods of time, to notice your body sensations, and to end or reduce negative thoughts and feelings (Davis and Hayes 2011). Having the ability to practice calming the mind and body has a long list of benefits that only the individual can identify.

In his biography, Steve Jobs, the brain behind the iPhone and many other technological devices, talked about using mindfulness meditation to calm the mind and body for creative purposes. He noted how restless his mind would get, and that if he tried to calm it, sometimes the restlessness would get worse. He found—and you will too—that over time, your mind can calm down (Isaacson 2011). Once your mind is calm, things become clearer. Katie found this to be true in her experience with mindfulness meditation.

> *I couldn't sit still for even a minute at first. My mind kept racing with thoughts of my mom. I followed along, though, and just let the thoughts go. Every. Single. One. Every single time. It was hard, but I noticed even after the first time that I did feel calmer—better somehow.*

Wrap-Up

Though many of the activities in this book are meant to calm your body and your mind; move you out of a state of stress and anxiety; and release the fight, flight, freeze, faint response, this chapter focused specifically on calming the body's stress reactions by scanning the body and noticing sensations and feelings in the moment. Practices such as mindfulness meditation teach us how to ease the stressful thoughts and feelings in our mind. Practicing—not finishing or winning—is the important part of mindfulness meditation; practice will help you feel how mindfulness meditation calms the body and mind.

Finding ways to calm your body; ease your mind; and let go of thoughts and feelings that bring anxiety, fear, sadness, and anger is part of leading a healthy life. Doing these things for your body and mind is not the same as avoiding or denying feelings and thoughts; rather, you are learning how to return your body and mind to a state of calm.

What's Next?

We end the book by looking once again at the whole body from the perspective of health and healing. Chapter 10 continues the approach of helping you find ways to get balance and return you and your body to that state of health and well-being that is its natural home. Finding hope and meaning in loss is an important part of healing—and even enjoying life—as you move through grief.

chapter 10

your healing body

I never thought it would happen—that I'd laugh and be happy again, that I wouldn't be sad all the time, that I'd heal from her death.

—Emma

I've hurt a lot, I've learned a lot, and I'm better, from both the hurt and the lessons I've learned.

—Matt

I'll never get over losing her, but I am getting through it. I didn't do it alone; no one can.

—Katie

Like Emma and so many grieving teens, it is hard to imagine ever healing from something that hurts so much. However, your body is designed to heal—even a broken heart, even a traumatized brain on fight, flight, freeze, faint alert. Your body and your brain are meant to find *homeostasis*, a natural state of balance in which both are in their healthiest states—even after the traumatic loss of a loved one.

Stress is the most significant biological factor that creates imbalance in our body and our emotions. We've learned what stress can do to our muscles, our brains, our breathing, and our heart rate. It can be hard to imagine ever getting back to home base when it seems to have moved. Like Katie said, you don't get over grief, you get through it. And you don't do it alone. With help and support and advice, and by practicing the healthy strategies in this book, you can find ways to cope with loss and get your life back in balance. Here are two activities to help you deal with day-to-day challenges even in the most stressful "storms."

10.1 The Rule of Threes to Deal with Stress

For basic survival (especially during those first few days of grieving), every day:

1. Brush your teeth and hair, but not with the same brush! (You need to retain your sense of humor...)

2. Eat something every three hours. (Be sure it isn't total junk food, like what you get from a vending machine or gas station.)

3. Breathe three deep breaths. (Any time you're overwhelmed, anxious, confused, tired, angry, or happy, just take the time to take it all in with three deep breaths.)

For basic sanity (just to keep from losing control of your life), every day:

1. Pick *just* three things to get done at school. (Try to make it the three most important or the three that are due now.)

2. Pick *just* three things to get done at home or with your friends. (Yes, calling your best friend can be one of the three things.)

3. Pick *just* three things you are going to take *off* that list of all the stuff you have to do (or should do, or someone wants you to do).

For basic steadiness (to keep your life in balance), every day:

1. Start with three intentions. (These are not more things to do; rather, they are emotions and thoughts about how you wish your day would go.)

2. In the middle of the day, stop for three minutes. (That's it! Just stop doing stuff and "be" for three minutes.)

3. End your day thinking of three good things, and be grateful for them—and whatever else you can think of. (See activity 7.2, three good things, for help with this one.)

Breaking your day and grief down into threes can make the work of healing a little simpler. Ending your days with something to look forward to or to be grateful for helps you sleep better, reduces stress, and starts the next day off better.

10.2 Roots Pose with the Winds of Grief

Practicing this yoga pose is a great way to start your day, improving your strength, your balance, and your sense of meaning. But first, go back and review and practice activity 6.4 (forward fold), and begin in mountain pose.

1. While in mountain pose, imagine that each foot has four strong roots growing out of it: one at the base of your big toe, one at the

base of your pinky toe, one along the inner edge of your heel, and one along the outer edge of your heel.

2. Picture these roots moving into the ground, growing thicker and stronger as they move through the earth. Imagine them going deep into the core of the earth, wrapping around the core and holding on tight. Feel your strength and balance now that you have roots.

3. Imagine a small wind picks up in your life, a little stressor such as not doing well on a test or having an argument with your best friend. Feel your body move just a little to the left and to the right, back and forth as your strong roots help you maintain balance.

4. Now imagine your grief at the beginning, how it nearly knocked you over; lean farther to the left and then to the right, back and forth. By keeping your roots strongly planted, you can maintain your balance even when the winds and storms of grief blow.

5. Take three deep breaths and remember the experience of having strong roots to keep your balance no matter what winds of change occur.

Finding Hope and Meaning

Finding some sort of meaning to life after a death is key to healing, to living life without the person you love. Emma struggled to find any meaning in the loss of her young sister. She described her life and her family as "broken," shattered even. She and her family were unsure of how or why to go on without their little Sophie.

It's as though we weren't whole anymore. There was a hole—a piece was missing from our lives, from our family. We were broken into a million pieces and were not sure how to get ourselves back together, or if we ever would.

Finding meaning in what has happened, in your family, in your life, and in your future is an important part of healing. You are different now that you have lost a loved one. The following activity beautifully illustrates the feeling of brokenness and how to put the pieces back together.

10.3 Beautiful in the Broken Places

Find a beautiful plate or bowl that you don't mind breaking. (Or that your parents don't mind you breaking!) Gently tap on the center of the piece with a small hammer or the back of a large metal spoon until there are about six broken pieces. You'll also need ceramic glue, a small paintbrush, and some shiny gold paint.

1. As you look at the broken pieces, understand that this once beautiful dish is now broken; it has changed and is not the same as it was. This broken dish represents your life since your loved one died.

2. Begin to glue the pieces back together. Take a minute to hold the pieces together as you glue them and consider everything that has been required for you to heal, to come back together.

3. Once all the pieces are in place, you can see that the dish is jagged and rough and scarred; it has changed permanently, but it is whole again.

4. Now, using the paintbrush and gold paint, paint each broken line of the dish. As you look at the dish now, can you see that it is beautiful? Despite the brokenness, both you and the dish are beautiful in the broken places.

Finding beauty again, even in the broken places, is what healing your grief means. In order to find it, you have to have a little bit of hope. *Hope* is the feeling that everything will be okay; there's a light somewhere in the darkness, a future is waiting—maybe not the one you thought, but the one you have, if you continue to have hope and believe that your life has meaning.

Wrap-Up

Getting life back in balance and finding meaning and hope in your life and your loss are the keys to healing your grieving heart and body. Finding what helps you cope, what relieves stress, and what calms your body and brain is how healing happens.

Your heart will always carry a bit of the hurt. Maybe there will always be a little hole there, but that doesn't mean your hurt has to take over your life. And just because you heal yourself, it doesn't mean that you somehow forget the person who died. Your loved one's memory is not dependent on the amount of pain you feel. You honor that person when you live life fully. Bringing a state of balance and calmness back into your life not only soothes your grief, it helps you remember your loved one clearly and with a sense of peace, even in your grief and loss.

epilogue: begin again

This book is coming to an end, but your grief is not. Each day when you wake up and realize that it's true, *my special person has died*, your grief or sadness or anger or loneliness may bubble back up or hit you between the eyes and knock you over. That's the way grief operates: it comes and goes like waves on the ocean, back and forth. On some days you will barely notice or remember you are grieving. On other days you will believe it may never be over.

Then you begin again. Take three deep breaths (again). Page through the activities in this book and do one you like, or try one you never did or one you didn't like the first time you tried it. Everything in life is about beginning again, moving forward, and making your way through its joy and heartbreak.

You will change and grow from this experience; there's no way to avoid it, just like there's no way to avoid your body and brain responding to the trauma and grief of loss. You can attempt to hide the grief and loss, avoid them, stuff them, and deny them, but your body will not let you forget that you have had a life-changing experience. Keep in mind that the feelings and thoughts around your grief and loss, like all feelings and thoughts, change; they don't last forever. How you behave around those ever-changing feelings and thoughts is a choice you make. Sometimes you make good choices, sometimes not; here too you have the opportunity to begin again. Make amends if you need to, notice how your body feels and what feelings or thoughts are bubbling up, and begin again.

Though grief, in many ways, is a solitary and individual experience, it is not healed alone. Find others traveling the same path; follow them, walk beside them, or lead the way. Just don't stop moving forward. Remember, you can begin again.

acknowledgments

Thank you to Wendy Millstine for seeing the value in my research and my way of helping grieving people. To Ryan Buresh, Clancy Drake, Marisa Solís, Caleb Beckwith, and James Lainsbury for holding my hand and editing my "pen" throughout this process. Thank you to New Harbinger Publications for taking up a lot of space on my bookshelves throughout the years with your cutting-edge, helpful, and hopeful books and authors. I am honored to be among you.

Thank you to Children's Grief Connection; to my coworkers, board members, volunteers, funeral directors, supporters; and mostly to the families we have served over the years. This book could not have been possible without my association with an organization and a group of people who really do bring hope and healing to grieving families and children.

Thank you to my teen "ghostwriter," editor, and good friend, Danielle Hogue. Dani's strength, intuition, grace, sense of humor, and incredible smile made up for her merciless edits on my grammar and punctuation and her candid, authentic commentary on my writing. You, Dani, are what makes me feel that the world my grandchildren will grow up in is in good hands.

appendix A: what's your trauma response?

Check each item that you have felt, thought, or done since your loved one died to see what type of trauma response you are likely experiencing.

Fight Responses

☐ Avoiding close relationships for fear of "going off"

☐ Tightening hands into fists, ready to punch or tear at something or someone

☐ Flexing or tightening the jaw, grinding teeth, or snarling at people

☐ Glaring at others with cold eyes

☐ Using a threatening voice or making verbal threats

☐ Wanting to stomp, kick, and smash with legs and feet

☐ Feeling anger that quickly moves to rage

☐ Experiencing homicidal or suicidal feelings and thoughts

☐ Feeling knots, burning sensations, or nausea in the stomach

☐ Feeling like a bomb or a volcano ready to erupt

Flight Responses

☐ Feeling restless, especially in the legs and feet

☐ Feeling numbness in the legs and feet

☐ Breathing shallowly

☐ Experiencing anxiety, excess worry, and a feeling that you're ready for the worst

☐ Scanning the environment constantly with wide, darting eyes

☐ Feeling fidgety and tense

☐ Feeling trapped or held in place

☐ Needing to run

☐ Moving from one activity to the next in an overactive manner

☐ Pursuing lots of physical exercise and movement

Freeze Responses

☐ Feeling stuck in some part of the body

☐ Feeling cold or frozen or numb

☐ Feeling stiff or heavy

☐ Experiencing feelings of dread and a pounding heart

☐ Noticing a decrease in heart rate

☐ Being always on the lookout for a threat

☐ Daydreaming or fantasizing

Faint Responses

☐ Lacking the ability to concentrate

☐ Feeling spacey

☐ Feeling like you're floating, as if you are looking down on what is happening

☐ Sensing a loss of time

☐ Feeling unable to concentrate

☐ Forgetting things

☐ Being unaware of surroundings several times a day

☐ Moving from one space to another without knowing how you got there

appendix B:
depression diagnosis
checklist

There are differences between grief and diagnosed depression, and not all grieving people will suffer from depression. Take a look at the chart that follows for help in understanding the differences. If you think you fall more into the depression category, continue on with the checklist that follows the table.

Grief	Depression
Feel sad but can switch to normal moods throughout the day	Feel sad and mad, sometimes at self, most of the day, most of the week
Experience changes in moods, activity level, appetite, and sleep	Consistently feel tired, lose appetite, have trouble sleeping, and may be hyperactive or aggressive
Express anger at appropriate times even if not in appropriate ways	Express anger in the form of rage or deny being angry at all
May feel guilty for somehow not preventing the death or be preoccupied with the loss	May be ashamed and see self as bad and worthless; preoccupied with self
Respond to warmth and reassurance from others; able to comfort self	May be unresponsive to others or respond only with pressure and urging
Able to experience pleasure at times, even laugh and feel happy	Rarely able to enjoy pleasure or laugh, feel unhappy most of the time

If you have been experiencing more than six of the symptoms below most of the day, every day, for at least a couple of weeks, have your parent make an appointment to see your doctor or a grief therapist to help determine if you are suffering from depression and what can be done to help.

- ☐ Constant sadness, anger, or irritability

- ☐ Nothing feels fun; don't even want to try and have fun

- ☐ Don't feel like doing any of the things you used to love to do

- ☐ Feel bad, worthless, guilty, ashamed, or "wrong"

- ☐ Chronic worry or constant fears

- ☐ Sleep too much or can't sleep at all

- ☐ Lots of physical symptoms, such as stomachaches, leg pain, joint ache, and headaches

- ☐ Don't feel hungry enough to eat, or eat all the time

- ☐ Feel hopeless and helpless

- ☐ Can't concentrate; grades are dropping in school

- ☐ Thinking about using alcohol or drugs to feel better

- ☐ Thinking about death or suicide

appendix C: suicide risk signs

As you review these signs for suicide risk, keep in mind that this is a general list of possible signs and risk factors. If you find yourself or a friend displaying many of these signs, get help right away.

- No sense of meaning or purpose to life

- Withdrawal from friends and family members

- Feeling trapped, like there's no way out of a situation

- If you feel you are in danger of hurting yourself or others because of your intense feelings, please tell someone. Ask for help. You don't need to feel this badly, and someone does want to help. National Suicide Prevention Lifeline: 800-273-TALK (8255). National Youth Crisis Hotline: 800-448-4663.

- Trouble in romantic relationships

- Difficulty getting along with others

- Acting rebellious and/or exhibiting high-risk behaviors

- Unusual gift giving or giving away of possessions

- Appearing bored or distracted

- Writing or drawing pictures about death

- Running away from home

- Dramatic personality changes

- Suddenly happier, calmer

- Changes in appearance and personal grooming, lacking concern

- History of previous suicide attempts

- Visiting or calling people unexpectedly

- Talk of suicide (even in a joking way)

references and
selected readings

Aan het Rot, M., K. A. Collins, and H. L. Fitterling. 2009. "Physical Exercise and Depression." *Mount Sinai Journal of Medicine* 76 (2): 204–14.

American Psychological Association. 2016. "Stress Effects on the Body." http://www.apa.org/helpcenter/stress-body.aspx.

Baenninger, R., S. Binkley, and M. Baenninger. 1996. "Field Observations of Yawning and Activity in Humans." *Physiology & Behavior* 59 (3): 421–25.

Bennett, D. A., J. A. Schneider, Y. Tang, S. E. Arnold, and R. S. Wilson. 2006. "The Effect of Social Networks on the Relation Between Alzheimer's Disease Pathology and Level of Cognitive Function in Old People: A Longitudinal Cohort Study." *The Lancet Neurology* 5 (5): 406–12.

Benson, H., B. R. Marzetta, B. A. Rosner, and H. M. Klemchuk. 1974. "Decreased Blood-Pressure in Pharmacologically Treated Hypertensive Patients Who Regularly Elicited the Relaxation Response." *The Lancet* 303 (7852). 289–91.

Benton, D., and R. T. Donohoe. 1999. "The Effects of Nutrients on Mood." *Public Health Nutrition* 2 (3a): 403–9.

Borkin, S. 2014. *The Healing Power of Writing: A Therapist's Guide to Using Journaling with Clients*. New York: W. W. Norton.

Bowlby, J. 1969. *Attachment and Loss*. Vol. 1. New York: Basic Books.

Bugge, K. E., K. T. S. Haugstvedt, E. G. Røkholt, P. Darbyshire, and S. Helseth. 2012. "Adolescent Bereavement: Embodied Responses,

Coping and Perceptions of a Body Awareness Support Programme." *Journal of Clinical Nursing* 21 (15–16): 2160–9.

Cherniack, E. P., and A. R. Cherniack. 2014. "The Benefit of Pets and Animal-Assisted Therapy to the Health of Older Individuals." *Current Gerontology and Geriatrics Research.* Available online at http://www.ncbi.nlm.nih.gov/pmc/articles/PMC4248608.

Children's Grief Awareness Day. n.d. "Did You Know? Children and Grief Statistics." https://www.childrensgriefawarenessday.org/cgad2/pdf/griefstatistics.pdf.

Crenshaw, D. A. 2007. "An Interpersonal Neurobiological-Informed Treatment Model for Childhood Traumatic Grief." *Omega* 54 (4): 319–35.

Cuddy, A. 2015. *Presence: Bringing Your Boldest Self to Your Biggest Challenges.* New York: Little, Brown and Company.

Davis, D. M., and J. A. Hayes. 2011. "What Are the Benefits of Mindfulness? A Practice Review of Psychotherapy-Related Research." *Psychotherapy* 48 (2): 198–208.

Emmons, H. 2010. *The Chemistry of Calm: A Powerful, Drug-Free Plan to Quiet Your Fears and Overcome Your Anxiety.* New York: Touchstone.

Felitti, V. J., R. F. Anda, D. Nordenberg, D. F. Williamson, A. M. Spitz, V. Edwards, M. P. Koss, and J. S. Marks. 1998. "Relationship of Childhood Abuse and Household Dysfunction to Many of the Leading Causes of Death in Adults: The Adverse Childhood Experiences (ACE) Study." *American Journal of Preventive Medicine* 14 (4): 245–58.

Flaxman, G., and L. Flook. n.d. *Brief Summary of Mindfulness Research.* Poster presented at the Center for Mindfulness in Medicine, Health Care, and Society 6th Annual Conference, Worcester, MA. Available at http://marc.ucla.edu/workfiles/pdfs/marc-mindfulness-research-summary.pdf.

Fogel, A. 2013. *Body Sense: The Science and Practice of Embodied Self-Awareness*. New York: W. W. Norton.

Fredrick, J. F. 1976. "Grief as a Disease Process." *Omega* 7 (4): 297–305.

Gedney, J. J., T. L. Glover, and R. B. Fillingim. 2004. "Sensory and Affective Pain Discrimination After Inhalation of Essential Oils." *Psychosomatic Medicine* 66 (4): 599–606.

Gillen, L., and J. Gillen. 2008. *Yoga Calm for Children: Educating Heart, Mind, and Body*. Portland, OR: Three Pebble Press.

Hansen, S. A. 2013. *The Executive Functioning Workbook for Teens: Help for Unprepared, Late, and Scattered Teens*. Oakland, CA: New Harbinger Publications.

Hanson, R., and R. Mendius. 2009. *Buddha's Brain: The Practical Neuroscience of Happiness, Love, and Wisdom*. Oakland, CA: New Harbinger Publications.

Holt-Lunstad, J., T. B. Smith, and J. B. Layton. 2010. "Social Relationships and Mortality Risk: A Meta-Analytic Review." *PLOS Medicine* 7 (7): 1–9.

Institute for Trauma and Stress at the NYU Child Study Center. 2002. *Caring for Kids After Trauma and Death: A Guide for Parents and Professionals*. Available online at http://www.nctsn.org/nctsn_assets/pdfs/Crisis%20Guide%20-%20NYU.pdf.

Isaacson, Walter. 2011. *Steve Jobs*. New York: Simon & Schuster.

Jerath, R., J. W. Edry, V. A. Barnes, and V. Jerath. 2006. "Physiology of Long Pranayamic Breathing: Neural Respiratory Elements May Provide a Mechanism That Explains How Slow Deep Breathing Shifts the Autonomic Nervous System." *Medical Hypotheses* 67 (3): 566–71.

Johns Hopkins Medicine Heart & Vascular Institute. n.d. "Stress Cardiomyopathy Symptoms and Diagnosis." http://www.hopkinsmedicine.org/heart_vascular_institute/conditions_treatments/conditions/stress_cardiomyopathy/symptoms_diagnosis.html.

Judd L. L., P. J. Schettler, W. Coryell, H. S. Akiskal, and J. G. Fiedorow-icz. 2013. "Overt Irritability/Anger in Unipolar Major Depressive Episodes: Past and Current Characteristics and Implications for Long-Term Course." *JAMA Psychiatry* 70 (11): 1171–80.

Kahn, P. H., Jr. 1997. "Developmental Psychology and the Biophilia Hypothesis: Children's Affiliation with Nature." *Developmental Review* 17: 1–61.

Kerr, D. C. R., D. T. Zava, W. T. Piper, S. R. Saturn, B. Frei, and A. F. Gombart. 2015. "Associations Between Vitamin D Levels and Depressive Symptoms in Healthy Young Adult Women." *Psychiatry Research* 227 (1): 46–51.

Koutsikou S., J. J. Crook, E. V. Earl, J. L. Leith, T. C. Watson, B. M. Lumb, and R. Apps. 2014. "Neural Substrates Underlying Fear-Evoked Freezing: The Periaqueductal Grey–Cerebellar Link." *Journal of Physiology* 592 (10): 2197–213.

Kross, E., M. G. Berman, W. Mischel, E. E. Smith, and T. D. Wager. 2011. "Social Rejection Shares Somatosensory Representations with Physical Pain." *Proceedings of the National Academy of Sciences* 108 (15): 6270–5.

Lazar, S. W., C. E. Kerr, R. H. Wasserman, J. R. Gray, D. N. Greve, M. T. Treadway et al. 2005. "Meditation Experience is Associated with Increased Cortical Thickness." *Neuroreport* 16 (17): 1893–7.

Leeds, A. M. 2009. *A Guide to the Standard EMDR Protocols for Clinicians, Supervisors, and Consultants.* New York: Springer.

Lehrner, J., G. Marwinski, S. Lehr, P. Johren, and L. Deecke. 2005. "Ambient Odors of Orange and Lavender Reduce Anxiety and Improve Mood in a Dental Office." *Physiology & Behavior* 86 (1–2): 92–5.

National Alliance for Grieving Children. 2011–2012. "National Poll of Bereaved Children and Teenagers." https://children grieve.org/index.php?q=national-poll-bereaved-children -teenagers.

Ogden, P., K. Minton, and C. Pain. 2006. *Trauma and the Body: A Sensorimotor Approach to Psychotherapy*. New York: W. W. Norton.

Owens, J. 2014. "Insufficient Sleep in Adolescents and Young Adults: An Update on Causes and Consequences." *Pediatrics* 134 (3): e921–32.

Parnell, L. 2008. *Tapping In: A Step-by-Step Guide to Activating Your Healing Resources Through Bilateral Stimulation*. Boulder, CO: Sounds True.

Patel, P. 2014. "A Study to Assess the Effectiveness of Progressive Muscle Relaxation Therapy on Stress Among Staff Nurses Working in Selected Hospitals at Vadodara City." *IOSR Journal of Nursing and Health Science* 3 (3): 34–59.

Pilling, J., B. K. Thege, Z. Demetrovics, and M. S. Kopp. 2012. "Alcohol Use in the First Three Years of Bereavement: A National Representative Survey." *Substance Abuse Treatment, Prevention, and Policy* 7: 3.

Popowitz, C. 2014. "Therapists' Perspective on the Use of Somatic Interventions in Childhood Trauma." *Master of Social Work Clinical Research Papers*, Paper 377. Available at http://sophia.stkate.edu/cgi/viewcontent.cgi?article=1380& context=msw_papers.

Reisen, D. 2014. "Helping the Body Grieve: A Body Psychotherapy Approach to Supporting the Creation of Continuing Bonds After a Death Loss." *International Body Psychotherapy Journal* 13 (1): 80–94.

Santa Clara University Cowell Center. n.d. "Relaxation Exercises." https://www.scu.edu/cowell/caps/getting-help-with -depression/stress-and-relaxation-interactive-program/level -two/relaxation-exercises.

Seligman, M. E., T. A. Steen, N. Park, and C. Peterson. 2005. "Positive Psychology Progress: Empirical Validation of Interventions." *American Psychologist* 60 (5): 410–21.

Siegel, D. J. 2013. *Brainstorm: The Power and Purpose of the Teenage Brain*. New York: Jeremy P. Tarcher/Penguin.

Siegel, D. J., and T. P. Bryson. 2012. *The Whole-Brain Child: 12 Revolutionary Strategies to Nurture Your Child's Developing Mind*. New York: Bantam Books.

Substance Abuse and Mental Health Services Administration. 2010. "Drug-Related Suicide Attempts: Teens and Young Adults." *SAMHSA News* 18 (4): 15. Available online at http://archive.samhsa.gov/samhsaNewsletter/Volume_18 _Number_4/JulyAugust2010.pdf.

Suicide Awareness Voices in Education (SAVE). http://www .save.org.

Utay, J., and M. Miller. 2006. "Guided Imagery as an Effective Therapeutic Technique: A Brief Review of Its History and Efficacy Research." *Journal of Instructional Psychology* 33 (1): 40–3.

Van der Kolk, B. 2014. *The Body Keeps the Score: Brain, Mind, and Body in Healing Trauma*. New York: Viking.

Van Middendorp, H., M. A. Lumley, J. W. Jacobs, L. J. van Doornen, J. W. Bijlsma, and R. Geenen. 2008. "Emotions and Emotional Approach and Avoidance Strategies in Fibromyalgia." *Journal of Psychosomatic Research* 64 (2): 159–67.

What's Your Grief? 2014. "64 Songs About Grief and Loss: Volume One." http://www.whatsyourgrief.com/songs-about -grief-and-loss.

Zajonc, R. B. 1989. "Styles of Explanation in Social Psychology." *European Journal of Social Psychology* 19 (5): 345–68.

Coral Popowitz, MSW, LGSW, is executive director of Children's Grief Connection, and has established a private practice working with children and families for over twenty-five years. She has presented at regional, national, and international conferences on the subjects of trauma and grief.

More Instant Help Books for Teens
An Imprint of New Harbinger Publications

STUFF THAT SUCKS
A Teen's Guide to Accepting
What You Can't Change &
Committing to What You Can

ISBN: 978-1626258655 / US $12.95

MINDFULNESS FOR
TEEN DEPRESSION
A Workbook for Improving
Your Mood

ISBN: 978-1626253827 / US $16.95

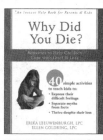

STOPPING THE PAIN
A Workbook for Teens Who
Cut & Self-Injure

ISBN: 978-1572246027 / US $16.95

COMMUNICATION SKILLS
FOR TEENS
How to Listen, Express &
Connect for Success

ISBN: 978-1626252639 / US $16.95

GRIEVING FOR THE
SIBLING YOU LOST
A Teen's Guide to Coping
with Grief & Finding
Meaning After Loss

ISBN: 978-1626252493 / US $16.95

WHY DID YOU DIE?
Activities to Help Children
Cope with Grief & Loss

ISBN: 978-1572246041 / US $19.95

newharbingerpublications
1-800-748-6273 / newharbinger.com

(VISA, MC, AMEX / prices subject to change without notice)

Follow Us   ◙ ⓟ

Don't miss out on new books in the subjects that interest you.
Sign up for our **Book Alerts** at **newharbinger.com/bookalerts**

Register your **new harbinger** titles for additional benefits!

When you register your **new harbinger** title—purchased in any format, from any source—you get access to benefits like the following:

- Downloadable accessories like printable worksheets and extra content
- Instructional videos and audio files
- Information about updates, corrections, and new editions

Not every title has accessories, but we're adding new material all the time.

Access free accessories in 3 easy steps:

1. Sign in at NewHarbinger.com (or **register** to create an account).

2. Click on **register a book**. Search for your title and click the **register** button when it appears.

3. Click on the **book cover or title** to go to its details page. Click on **accessories** to view and access files.

That's all there is to it!

If you need help, visit:

NewHarbinger.com/accessories

new harbinger
CELEBRATING
40 YEARS